Scripture for Meditation: 4

COLOSSIANS

by John Bligh

ST PAUL PUBLICATIONS

ST PAUL PUBLICATIONS
LANGLEY, BUCKS., GREAT BRITAIN.

SBN 85439 020 0

NIHIL OBSTAT:
RT. REV. MGR. R. J. FOSTER, S.T.L., L.S.S.

IMPRIMATUR:
✝ GEORGE PATRICK DWYER
    ARCHBISHOP OF BIRMINGHAM
BIRMINGHAM: 9TH SEPTEMBER 1969

FIRST PUBLISHED NOVEMBER 1969 BY ST PAUL PUBLICATIONS AND
PRINTED IN ENGLAND BY SOCIETY OF ST PAUL, LANGLEY, BUCKS.

CONTENTS

Foreword

St Paul's Epistle to the Colossians resembles in various ways his Epistle to the Philippians: in both the general tone is one of encouragement and thanksgiving; in both the apostle is at pains to set before his readers a worthy conception of the person and work of Christ; and in both he warns them against false doctrines, propagated by unnamed opponents, which will, if accepted, corrupt their faith and endanger their salvation. The chief difference between the two Epistles is that the members of the church of Colossae are not personally known to St Paul. He is writing to encourage a young community founded by one of his disciples named Epaphras.

This beautiful Epistle, replete with inspiration and instruction, deserves a more prominent place in the liturgy than it has had hitherto. Thanks to the developments encouraged by Vatican II, it now has a chance to come into its own.

John Bligh, S.J.

1

An Atmosphere
of Encouragement

A Prayer of Congratulation

From Paul, by the will of God an apostle of Jesus Christ, and the brother Timothy, to God's people at Colossae, our brethren through faith in Christ: grace and peace be upon you from God our Father.

We give thanks to God, the Father of our Lord Jesus Christ, every time we think of you in our prayers, for we have heard of your faith in Christ Jesus and of the charity which you bear to all God's people, a charity that springs from your hope for the blessings stored up for you in heaven, as you have heard in the message of truth which the gospel brought among you. It is the same everywhere: the gospel bears fruit and thrives the world over, as it has done among you, ever since the day when you first heard it and recognized it as being truly a grace offered you by God.

You were taught it by my beloved fellow-servant Epaphras, who has been a faithful servant of Christ on

my behalf. It is he who has told me of the charity inspired in you by the Holy Spirit. *(Col 1:1-8)*

An Encouraging Promise

Peter said to Jesus: 'Look at us! We have left everything and followed you! What will be our reward?' Jesus
answered them: 'I tell you truly, in the time of rebirth,
when the Son of Man takes his seat upon his throne of
glory, you too, who have been my followers, will sit on
twelve thrones as rulers of the twelve tribes of Israel.
And everyone who has left home or brothers or sisters
or father or mother or children or land for my name's
sake, will be rewarded many times over, and will gain
eternal life.' *(Mt 19:27-29)*

At the Last Supper

Jesus said to his disciples: 'You are the men who have
stayed with me through my trials. Therefore I covenant
to you the kingly power which my Father has covenanted
to me. You shall eat and drink at my table in the kingdom of God and sit on thrones ruling the twelve tribes
of Israel.' *(Lk 22:28-30)*

The Purpose of Preaching

Paul and his companions sailed from Paphos and went
to Perge in Pamphilia. Here John left their company
and returned to Jerusalem. The others went on from
Perge and reached Pisidian Antioch. On the sabbath they
went into the synagogue and sat down. After the read-
ings from the law and the prophets, the presidents of the
synagogue sent a message to them: 'Brethren, if you

have in you any words of encouragement for the people,
you may speak.' Paul came forward, raised his hand for
silence, and spoke.   (*Acts 13:13-16*)

Reflection

In books on the life and work of St Paul, his missionary
career is usually divided into three missionary journeys,
one before the Council of Jerusalem (A.D. 49) and the
other two after it, separated from each other by a further
visit to Jerusalem in 53 or 54 A.D. This is a convenient
way of viewing his work, but we must not imagine that
he was always journeying on and on, relentlessly, and
never staying still. Rather, his method was to go to the
administrative centre of a Roman province — Ephesus
in Asia, Thessalonica in Macedonia, Corinth in Achaea
— and stay there teaching for months or even years. He
left it to his disciples to carry the gospel up into the
hinterland of the provinces.

At the time of writing to the Colossians, he is in
prison again, perhaps in Rome, but more probably at
Ephesus, where he spent at least three months during
his third missionary journey. [1] While he was in prison,
one of his converts, Epaphras, came and told him that
he had founded a Christian community at Colossae in
Phrygia, and asked him to write a letter of encouragement to this new church, to strengthen its members in
the faith he had taught them. The Epistle to the Colossians is St Paul's letter to this young community,
which he has never visited (cf. 2: 1).

-----

[1] Ephesus is more likely than Rome, because Colossians was
written from the same place as Philemon (see below, pp.
114-116). The slave Onesimus, on whose behalf Paul writes
to Philemon, is more likely to have fled from Colossae to
Ephesus than to Rome.

The Epistle contains warnings against false doctrines and 'philosophic' corruptions of the gospel. The conclusion (4:12-13) shows that Epaphras, for some reason, was deeply concerned about the danger. No doubt St Paul shared his solicitude, but in most parts of the Epistle the note of warning is not predominant. St Paul is sending words of congratulation and encouragement to the new community. The opening passage has the literary form of a prayer of thanks, but it is written down in order to be 'overheard' by the Colossians. Public prayer of this kind is not addressed to God alone; it is meant to instruct and encourage the bystanders at the same time. The Colossians will be pleased to know that Paul speaks so highly of them when he turns to God in prayer — that he recognizes their faith, hope and charity, and thanks God for these gifts. Paul is obliquely praising the Colossians and, at the same time, unobtrusively praising the gospel which they have accepted: it is bearing fruit and going from strength to strength the world over. What is more, thanks to their acceptance of the gospel, the Colossians can look forward to an inheritance in heaven.

This is how the Apostle creates an atmosphere of encouragement in the churches. He praises the virtues of faith, hope and charity which he sees in them, he praises the gospel itself, and he points to a glorious future. Christ our Lord did the same when encouraging his disciples: he praised them for staying with him in trying circumstances, and promised them a heavenly reward for their self-sacrifice in this world. The Holy Spirit, whose coming Christ promised, is a 'Paraclete' in several senses; among other things, he is an Encourager. In the Epistle to the Colossians, he is speaking through Paul to encourage a young church.

Immediately after Vatican II, the whole Church passed through a period of intense self-criticism, which was in many ways destructive. We cannot live permanently in such an atmosphere. There are now numerous signs that Christians prefer to listen to preachers who can utter a word of encouragement. We must cease to be intimidated by the word 'triumphalism'. St Paul's statement that the gospel thrives the world over might be described by a hostile critic as a piece of triumphalism. But because he said this kind of thing, the gospel did triumph. A cheerful, hopeful atmosphere of encouragement and even of mutual congratulation is necessary if any collective enterprise is to flourish. Self-denigration and defeatism, on the other hand, are not fruits of the Spirit.

When St Paul went into the synagogue at Antioch in Pisidia, the presidents sent him a message which showed great wisdom: 'If you have any words of encouragement for the people, you may speak.' They asked for the right thing — a word of encouragement for the people of God.

Prayer

Heavenly Father, open our eyes to see and appreciate the goodness of others; and let us not be too shy to express our approval, and to encourage one another in your service. May your Holy Spirit recreate an atmosphere of encouragement and hope throughout the Church.

2

Praying for Others

For Progress and Perseverance

From the day when I first heard of you, I have never ceased to pray for you. I pray that you may receive that fulness of spiritual wisdom and understanding which brings perfect knowledge of God's will, so that your manner of life may be worthy of the Lord and pleasing to him in every way. I pray that you may bear fruit in every good work as you advance in the knowledge of God. I pray that through his glorious power God will fill you with all strength to face the future with endurance, with fortitude, and with joyful gratitude to the Father who has made us fit to share the inheritance of his people in the kingdom of light.   (*Col 1:9-12*)

For Spiritual Gifts

Do not ask, 'What are we going to eat?' or 'What are we going to drink?' or 'What are we going to wear?' Those are the things the Gentiles are bent upon. Do not give way to anxiety, for your heavenly Father is aware that

14

you need all these things. Seek first the kingdom of God and his justice; then all these things will be given to you in addition. (*Mt 6:31-33*)

For Gifts Received

The seventy-two came back full of joy. 'Lord,' they said, 'even the devils submit to us when we use your name!' Jesus replied: 'I was watching Satan — he fell like a lightning-flash from heaven. You see now that I have given you power to trample on snakes and scorpions and to triumph over all the power of the enemy; nothing will do you harm. Rejoice, then, but not because spirits submit to you; rather, because your names are enrolled in heaven.'

At that time Jesus was filled with the joy of the Holy Spirit and said: 'I thank you, Father, Lord of heaven and earth, because you have hidden these things from the wise and the shrewd and revealed them to the simple; yes, Father, I thank you because this has been your good pleasure.

'Everything has been entrusted to me by my Father; no one knows who the Son is except the Father, or who the Father is except the Son, and those to whom the Son chooses to reveal him.'

Turning to the disciples, he said to them in private: 'Blessed are the eyes that see what you are seeing! I tell you, many prophets and kings desired to see the things that you are seeing and did not see them, and to hear the things that you are hearing and did not hear them.' (*Lk 10:17-24*)

For Protection and Consecration

Holy Father, keep them in your Name, these whom you gave me, that they may be one, as we are one. So long as I was with them, I watched over them in your Name, which you gave me; I protected them, and none of them perished except the one who is destined to be lost, for the Scripture must be fulfilled. Now I am on my way to you; but while I am still in the world, I speak these words, in order that they may have my joy in their hearts in full measure. I have given them your word. The world has come to hate them, because they are not of the world, as I am not of the world. Consecrate them in the truth, the truth which is your word.   (*Jn 17:11-17*)

Reflection

It was part of St Paul's apostolic and priestly ministry to pray for the churches which he and his converts founded. The first eleven verses of this Epistle give us a good idea of how he used to pray for them, both in his private prayers and in the liturgy, when he was free to attend and lead it.

In accordance with the rule which he gives in the Epistle to the Philippians (4:6), he joins petition with thanksgiving. Looking to the past, and contemplating God's abundant gifts to the Colossians, he pours out a fine prayer of thanksgiving from his joyful heart. The Christian liturgy has been called, from the beginning, 'the Eucharist', and the Greek word 'Eucharist' means 'Thanksgiving'. Gratitude should be the keynote of the liturgy — as indeed of the whole Christian life.

Because St Paul lives for others and loves them sincerely, he rejoices over God's gifts to *them*. His prayers, both of thanksgiving and of petition, are unselfish, priestly prayers. He is following the example of Christ, who in the passages from St Luke and St John, thanks his Father for the gift of wisdom given to his disciples, and prays that they may be sanctified by the truth which he has revealed, consecrated to it, and dedicated to its propagation.

In the passage from the Sermon on the Mount (Mt 6), Jesus tells his disciples not to seek in prayer the things of this world; and from Luke 10 it would seem that they are not even to seek miraculous powers of exorcism. They are to ask for heavenly gifts — the kingdom and its justice. That is what St Paul does: he prays that the Colossians may abound in knowledge of God's plans and of his will (sketched in v. 12), that they may advance in virtue and 'fruitfulness', and that they may persevere in their faith not wearily but with joy. If they understand all that God has done for them, they will be deeply grateful to him; being grateful, they will try to 'walk worthily'; sharing in the treasures of wisdom and knowledge offered by Christ, they will know how to walk worthily; and trusting in God the Father, they will find themselves able (or 'sufficient') to walk worthily. Men have only to seek understanding and fit themselves into God's plans; he will do the rest.

Every Christian can share in the apostolic work of the Church by imitating St Paul's prayer for other people. Christ's paradox, that 'he who loves his life will lose it, and he who hates it will preserve it' (Jn 12:25), can be applied to prayer. We must not concentrate solely on our own spiritual advancement when we pray; we should pray as members of the Body which is the Church, and forget ourselves in order to care for and pray for the other members. In the long run, this is best for one's own soul. In prayer we seek, among other things, self-understanding and adjustment to God's will; but his will is that we should understand ourselves as members of a Body, and other members as more important than ourselves (cf. Phil 2:3). Even in prayer, we must take the humble stance of a servant of others.

B

Prayer

Teach me, O heavenly Father, to put aside self-concern, even in my prayers, and to seek spiritual gifts, chiefly for other people, while I trust your Fatherly care to look after my own soul. Give us understanding, fill us with wonder at your goodness, and move us to express our gratitude in joyful obedience to your will.

3

Gratitude
to God our Saviour

The New Exodus

Let us give thanks to the Father who has made us fit to
share the inheritance of his people in the kingdom of
light. For he has rescued us from the domain of darkness,
and set us in the kingdom of his beloved Son, in whom
we have received redemption, the forgiveness of our sins.
(Col 1:12-14)

The God of Freedom

I am the Lord your God, who brought you out of the
land of Egypt, out of the house of bondage. You shall
have no other gods before me. *(Exod 20:2-3)*

Darkness and Light

God so loved the world that he gave his only Son, in order
that everyone who believes in him may not perish but

have eternal life. For God sent his Son into the world, not to condemn the world, but that the world might be saved through him. He who believes in him escapes condemnation; he who does not believe is condemned already, because he has not believed in the name of the only Son of God. This is the Judgment: the Light has come into the world and men have preferred darkness to the Light, because of their evil works.   (*Jn 3:16-19*)

Reflection

In this brief passage of the Epistle, St Paul speaks of the principal reason we have for gratitude to God — our redemption from the Egyptian darkness of sin into the kingdom of light and grace. Our redemption is a greater reason for gratitude than our creation, for 'it would have profited us nothing to be born, if we had not the blessing of rebirth' (Paschal Preface). The value of our existence is not to be estimated by surveying this life alone.

Just as Jesus in St John's gospel describes our redemption as a manifestation of the love of God the Father, so too does St Paul. It would be a travesty of the gospel to say that the merciful Christ rescued us from the wrath of God the Father, as though the two Persons were at discord. Jesus himself says (Jn 14:9): 'He who sees me sees the Father.' In all that he said and did Jesus revealed the Father. In redeeming us, he revealed the Father's love and desire to redeem us. Therefore our gratitude for the gift of redemption must always go back through the Son to the Father.

While writing this passage, St Paul was probably thinking of the Exodus from Egypt into the Promised Land as a type or figure of our redemption in Christ. The Jews still look back to the Exodus as the time of their liberation and think of God as the God of freedom. The command which the Lord sent to Pharaoh was: 'Let my people go, that they may serve me' (Exod 7:16), that is, 'Set them free, so that they may serve me in freedom.' At the beginning of the commandments, God reminds the Israelites that he is the God who freed them from the house of bondage. Gratitude for this benefit received should keep them faithful to the commandments which follow.

At Sinai itself, however, Israel fell into sin, by worshipping the Golden Calf. In punishment, God placed upon his people a burdensome ceremonial law, to preserve them from further sins of idolatry. They lost the freedom of the sons of God (cf. Exod 4:22) and were reduced to a condition which, in the eyes of Paul after his conversion, was a state of servitude — slavery to sin, and subjection to law (cf. Gal 4:1-3).

In the fulness of time, God sent forth his Son, to redeem those under the law — to liberate both Jew and Gentile from the darkness and bondage of sin, and to give them a share with his Son in the promised rest and the promised kingdom. This is the great blessing of 'redemption' for which Christians must constantly give thanks to the Father in the liturgy. They are released from the ceremonial law of the Jews (circumcision, food regulations, observance of new moons, etc.), but not of course from the decalogue. The ten commandments, given to Israel, God's first-born son, before the sin of the Golden Calf, are admonitions of a loving Father to his sons. Christians will obey them out of gratitude for their redemption. Christ enables us to fulfil them willingly and in the spirit in which they were given, both by explaining their meaning to us, and by strengthening us with his Holy Spirit.

The chief difference between these verses of the Epistle and the passage from St John is that whereas the evangelist is appealing for faith, St Paul is inviting us to join in an act of gratitude which presupposes faith. It is good that we should explicitly renew our decision to believe by making formal acts of faith; but perhaps faith is more perfect where it is simply taken for granted as a basis for gratitude, which completes the right relationship with God established through faith. Like faith, gratitude is a gift of God. In all things he takes the initiative. What is required of us is first humbly to accept his grace, and secondly to be grateful for it.

Gratitude is the middle term, or stepping-stone, from justification to Christian conduct. Because of all that God our Father has done for us we are grateful; and because we are grateful, we try to live as God our Father wants us to live — that is, in charity, joy and peace. So long as we live in this spirit, we have no need of a strict law with fearsome sanctions attached. We need only be told what is our Father's will, and we obey gladly and willingly. That is what St Paul means when he says (Rom 6:14): 'We are no longer under law, but under grace.' This can be illustrated by a rather crude comparison. I was once staying at Barmouth in North Wales. Between the house and the sea there was a primitive level-crossing with a gate which you opened for yourself. On the gate was an old cast-iron notice, left over from Victorian times, saying: 'Penalty for leaving gate open forty shillings', and across the top bar of the gate some more recent hand had daubed in white paint: 'Please shut the gate.' The man who is under law shuts the gate in order to avoid the fine; the man who is under grace shuts it because as soon as it is pointed out to him (if not before) he sees that this is the right and reasonable thing to do.

If we are truly grateful to God, first of all we will obey him willingly and gladly, as soon as we know what is his will. Secondly, if we are truly grateful to God, we will express our gratitude in prayer — because gratitude which does not express itself is worthless. And thirdly, if we are truly grateful, we will be eager to spread the faith to other people, to bring them to share the inheritance of God's people in the kingdom of light.

Prayer

We render thanks, almighty Father, for our redemption and liberation. Release us from the power of sin and from its attraction, so that we may observe your commandments gladly. Increase our love, for, to those who love you, your commandments are not grievous.

4

Christ
the Image of God

Who is Jesus?

He is the visible likeness of the invisible God, born
before all creation; for through him everything in heaven
and on earth, things visible and invisible, thrones, lordships, powers and authorities — all were created through
him and for him. Before all things were, he is; and all
things are held in being by him.   (*Col 1:15-17*)

Who sees me, sees the Father

Some men brought a paralytic lying on a bed. Jesus saw
their faith and said to the paralytic: 'Courage, my child;
your sins are forgiven.' At this, some of the scribes
thought to themselves: 'He is blaspheming!' Jesus knew
what they were thinking, and said: 'Why do you think
evil in your hearts? Which is easier: to say, "Your sins
are forgiven", or to say, "Rise up and walk"? However,
to show you that the Son of Man has power on earth to

forgive sins (then he turned to the paralytic): Rise up, take your bed, and go home.' He rose up and went home. When the people saw this, they were struck with awe and praised God for having given such power to men.

(Mt 9:2-8)

The Pre-Existent Christ

I have glorified you on earth by completing the work which you gave me to do. And now, Father, glorify me at your side with the glory which I had with you before the world began . . .

Father, my prayer for these whom you have given me is that where I am going to be, they too may be with me, that they may see the glory which you gave me, because you loved me, before the world's creation.

(Jn 17:4-5,24)

Reflection

One characteristic of the Epistles to the Colossians and to the Ephesians is what is known as their 'high Christology'. The rather clumsy word 'Christology' means 'an account of Christ', that is, an answer to the question, Who is Christ? [1] The question was raised by Jesus himself at Caesarea Philippi (Mk 8:27): 'Who do men say that I am?'

The New Testament contains several answers to this question, or in other words, several Christologies: 'He is a prophet,' 'He is the Son of Man,' 'He is the Suffering

---

[1] This question is itself clumsy. The real question is: 'Who is Jesus?' One answer is 'He is the Christ.' The question 'Who is Christ?' presupposes its own answer. It is like asking, What day is it on Sunday?

Servant,' 'He is the High Priest of the order of Mel-
chisedek,' 'He is the Christ, the Son of the living God.'
All these answers are correct, and none of them exhausts
the mystery; but some are more adequate than others.
A less adequate Christology is called by theologians a
'low Christology' (for example: Jesus is the prophet from
Galilee). A more adequate Christology is called a 'high
Christology' (for example: Jesus is the Son of God).

The highest Christology in the New Testament is
found in the prologue of St John, which says explicitly
that Jesus was and is God: 'In the beginning was the
Word, and the Word was with God, and the Word was
God....And the Word became flesh, and dwelt among
us.' Next highest come the prologue of the Epistle to
the Hebrews and this present passage of Colossians,
where Jesus is described as God's beloved Son, as the
Image of the invisible God, as existing before creation,
and as active in creating and sustaining the whole of
creation, including the angelic powers.

In the scene at the synagogue in Capharnaum, where
Jesus cures the paralytic, to unbelievers he seems a blas-
phemer. In forgiving sins, he acts as if he were God, for
who can forgive sins but God himself? But in the eyes
of the believer, he is the Image of God; the fulness of
the Godhead is present in him (cf. Col 2:9); it is by an
exercise of divine power that he justifies the paralytic,
and by the same power he cures him.

We cannot be sure exactly when Jesus first revealed
his pre-existence to his disciples. At all events, he speaks
openly of it in his Prayer at the Last Supper. If anyone
wishes to hold that this Prayer is a theological composi-
tion of the fourth evangelist rather than a report of what
Jesus actually said at the Last Supper, he should offer
some other explanation of the origin of the apostles' belief
in Jesus' pre-existence. But for those of us who are con-
vinced that the few simple things which Jesus said in the

highly charged atmosphere of the Last Supper burned themselves into the memories of those present, there is no difficulty: the disciples learned of the pre-existence of Christ from his own words.

St Paul introduces these high doctrines here in order to set before the eyes of his readers a worthy image of Christ the Lord whose name they have learned to invoke. Jesus is not to be pictured as a winsome young rabbi who 'roamed the hills of Galilee on a sad-eyed, lop-eared donkey' (Renan), but as the eternal Son of God, Lord of all by right of creation, and Lord again by right of redemption and re-creation. It was this great cosmic figure who emptied himself of the glory which he had with the Father before the world began, and took the form of a servant, in order to wash away our sins. He served us throughout his ministry and passion, and continues to serve us in the Church, working in and through his apostles and disciples.

But why does St Paul set this very high Christology before the Colossians in particular? Some extremely complicated answers have been given to this question, but probably the correct answer is very simple. St Paul, in prison, pictures this small, rather isolated little Christian community at Colossae, and wants to help them to realize what this thing is — the Church, of which they have become a part. (A second characteristic, by the way, of the Epistles to the Colossians and Ephesians is that when St Paul talks about 'the Church', he is talking about the universal Church, not the local church.) He wants this little group of converts to know that the Church with a capital C, of which they are now a part, is not just a loose network of small groups of people who venerate the memory of a certain Jewish rabbi and try to obey his teaching. It is a body of people who are here and now in living contact with this great cosmic figure of Christ who lives and reigns with God the Father. He is the source of power which sustains the universe; and to be united with him in faith is to be re-created and re-energized by him in a new way.

That is what we too have to thank God for: that we are not at enmity with the ground of our own being, but are reconciled with the heart of the universe, in which is made available to us a source of new power and strength and goodness and holiness. All that is required of us is to plug in to this source of power by saying: 'Take, O Lord, and receive my whole liberty, my memory, my understanding and my whole will — take them and energize them with your love and your grace.'

Prayer

Almighty and everlasting God, who sent your beloved Son to be the first-born among many brethren, grant that while we contemplate in him the visible image of your Godhead, we may be made worthy of our sonship.

5

Christ the Creator

Creator and Sustainer

He is the visible Image of the invisible God, born before
all creation; for through him everything in heaven and
on earth, things visible and invisible, thrones, lordships,
powers and authorities — all were created through him
and for him. Before all things were, he is; and all things
are held in being by him.   (*Col 1:15-17*)

Long ago, God gave many fragmentary revelations in a
variety of ways to our forefathers through the prophets;
but now in these last days he has spoken to us through
one who is his Son, whom he has made heir to the
universe, the Son through whom he created the ages.
This Son, who is the splendour of God's glory and the
full expression of his being, who sustains the universe
by his powerful word, after making atonement for sins,
has taken his seat at the right hand of the Almighty on
high, raised as far above the angels as the dignity which
he has inherited is greater than theirs.   (*Heb 1:1-4*)

The Secret of his Power

It was for deeds which Jesus did on the sabbath that the Jews began to persecute him. But he replied by saying: 'My Father is always at work, and so too am I.' Then the Jews were all the more determined to kill him, because, besides breaking the law of the sabbath, he was appropriating God as his own Father, and making himself equal to God.

Jesus replied: 'I tell you truly, a son cannot do anything by himself; he does only what he sees his father doing; for what the father does, that the son does too. The Father loves his Son and shows him all these things that he is doing; and he will show him even greater works than these, to fill you with wonder. For as the Father raises the dead and gives them life, so also the Son gives life to men according to his will; and the Father does not condemn anyone, but has entrusted all judgment to his Son; for it is his will that all should honour the Son no less than they honour the Father. He who refuses honour to the Son is refusing honour to the Father who sent him. (*Jn 5:16-23*)

Reflection

St Paul tells the Colossians, and the author of the Epistle to the Hebrews (doubtless a disciple of Paul) tells his readers, that Jesus is not only the pre-existing Image and likeness of the Father, but shared with him the work of creation and with him continues to sustain and contain the universe — to hold it in being and hold it together. The two chief questions presented by these texts are: How did the writers come to know this? And why do they mention the matter here?

To the first question, there are three possible answers, all of which may be correct. One is that Jesus revealed himself to his disciples as the Wisdom of God in such sayings as the Offer of the Easy Yoke.[1] Then the disciples, knowing that Wisdom was at work with God in creation (cf. Prov 8:27-31) and 'fills the world' and 'holds all things together' (Wis 1:7), inferred that Jesus, the pre-existent Son, was at work with his Father in creation and continues to hold all things together.

Secondly, those of us who accept the passage from John 5 as a reliable report of things which Jesus actually said to the Jews during his ministry, can say that Jesus himself revealed in his sabbath-day miracles and his explanations of them that the secret of his miraculous powers lay in his filial relationship to the Father. As any father teaches his craft to his son, so, Jesus says, God the Father taught his Son to perform the divine activities of giving life and passing judgment. These activities, which transcend the law and cannot be regulated by any law, are exercises of divine power. They belong to Jesus, because, as God's Son, he has the divine power.

Thirdly, since the glory of Christ is identical with his power, it is possible that when Peter, James and John saw his glory in the Transfiguration, and when Paul saw his glory on the road to Damascus, they somehow 'saw' that all things are sustained by Christ's power. St Paul says that he learned his gospel directly from Christ, in this vision (cf. Gal 1:12).

When 'Solomon' says that Wisdom, the Spirit of God, fills the world and holds all things together, he does so to draw a moralizing lesson: the Spirit, being everywhere, knows every word that is ever spoken. Hence no uncharitable word goes unobserved; murmuring is noticed, and punished with death (cf. Num 21:4-6). St

---

[1] Cf. *Scripture for Meditation 3: Our Divine Master,* pp. 14, 23.

Paul, however, draws no immediate moral. His purpose is in part to give the Colossians an exalted picture of Christ, and in part to prepare the way for the lesson which he will develop later: that we who are united to Christ by faith have no need to venerate the angels who gave the Jewish law. They too are Christ's creatures, and he has stripped them of power by his death (cf. Col 2:20; Gal 4:3,9).

But perhaps St Paul is also preparing the way for the whole body of moral instruction which is a necessary part of the gospel. His contemporary, Philo of Alexandria, had declared that Moses was the Logos or Wisdom of God. [1] 'Not so,' says St Paul, 'Christ is the Wisdom of God — in him are the treasures of wisdom and knowledge; it is he who can teach us how we must live in order to please God.' Indeed, the Christology of Colossians resembles certain ancient theories of the meaning and purpose of kingship, according to which the king, as a superior being, is able to contemplate and imitate the goodness of God, and his people become Godlike by imitating their king (i.e., God in his visible Image). This ideal, which is sometimes achieved imperfectly in 'ordinary' kings and queens, was fully realized in Christ. As the Christian is progressively filled with Christ's wisdom (1:9), he becomes able to walk more worthily and in a manner more pleasing to God (1:10).

Prayer

Grant, O heavenly Father, that we may see with the eyes of faith the glory of your Son throughout the world in which we live and move and have our being. Inspire us to pay him due reverence, and preserve us from vexing his kindly Spirit.

---

[1] Cf. *Galatians,* pp. 311-312.

6

The Primacy of Christ

Double First

He is the visible Image of the invisible God, born before all creation; for through him everything in heaven and on earth, things visible and invisible, thrones, lordships, powers and authorities — all were created through him and for him. Before all things were, he is; and all things are held in being by him. He is, too, the head of the body which is the Church — he who is its beginning, the first of the dead to be reborn. Thus in everything his rank is preeminent. It pleased God to place all perfection in him, and through him to reconcile the universe to himself.   (*Col 1:15-20*)

Angels Bypassed

It was fitting that God, the end and origin of creation, who has begun to lead many sons to glory, should bring to perfection through suffering the one who was to be their leader to salvation. (For the one who sanctifies and those who are sanctified are all alike from one stock.)

C

That is why he is not ashamed to call them his brothers, when he says: 'I shall proclaim your name to my brothers; in the midst of the Church I shall hymn your praises,' and again: 'I shall place my trust in him,' and again: 'Here am I, and here are the children whom God has given me.' Since, then, these 'children' are all kindred, all of the same flesh and blood, he too became part of that kindred, in order to render powerless, through his death, the one who has the power of death (that is, the devil), and so free those whom fear of death kept bound in slavery throughout their life. For it is not the angels that he took to himself, but the issue of Abraham.

(Heb 2:10-16)

God with us in the Church

The eleven disciples made the journey to Galilee, to the mountain where Jesus had told them to meet him. When they saw him they worshipped him, though some remained doubtful. Then Jesus drew near and addressed them: 'All power has been given to me in heaven and on earth,' he said. 'Go, then, and convert all the nations: baptize them in the name of the Father and of the Son and of the Holy Spirit, and teach them to observe all the commandments I have given you. And be sure, I am with you always, even to the end of the world.'

(Mt 28:16-20)

Reflection

In this passage of the Epistle, St Paul describes something of the mystery of the Church. It is a body of men and women whose head, Christ, is no ordinary man. He is 'first' and preeminent in two ways: he is God's first-born Son, and he is the first of the dead to be raised to life — to the new, indestructible life of the world to come. Although he is God's first-born Son, he is not a creature; along with the Father he is the Creator by whom all things were made. Before creation he possessed the 'fulness' of the divine wisdom, power and glory. This fulness came to dwell in the form of *man*, in unity of person.

Here is a mystery which the Epistle to the Hebrews makes more explicit: the angels were bypassed. When the Godhead came to dwell in a creature, no angelic creature was chosen. God took to himself a son of Abraham. He entered into a unique alliance or union with man, the closest analogy to which in our experience is the marriage alliance whereby two persons of different families step out of the sphere of their own families to some extent, in order to form a new family. The 'marriage' of God and man in Christ is an act of condescension on God's part, while man's dignity is correspondingly enhanced. God made his creation in order to love it; then, in his love for it, he overcame the distance between Creator and creature. 'What is man that thou art mindful of him?' asked the psalmist, 'or the son of man that thou dost care for him?' There is a story in Greek mythology of a sculptor who carved a statue of the most beautiful woman he could imagine; he then asked the gods to give his statue life, which they did, and then he married her. It is a parable for us of the assumption by God's Son of the human nature which he had created. The Incarnation itself, quite apart from the redemptive death of Christ, is a proof of God's desire to bring man close to himself in a union of love and a communion of life.

To be a member of Christ's Church is to be a member of his Body and share in his life — a life which has passed through death into the sphere of resurrection. All power is given to him in heaven and on earth — every angelic power and every human power is inferior to his.

To become a member of the Church is to open oneself to the influence of his beneficent power. It is to accept his teaching and with it the divine assistance which renders its fulfilment possible. The powers of the world to come are already at work in believers even during our mortal life. Thanks to Christ, we can begin to lead a heavenly life even on this earth.

Prayer

We believe, Lord Jesus, in your divinity and power, and want to receive the gifts which we believe you want to give us. Work powerfully, O Lord, in this community of which we are members, so that it may be recognized as a temple of your Holy Spirit, both by us who are its members, and by those outside.

7

Reconciliation

Estrangement Overcome

It pleased God to place all perfections in him, and
through him to reconcile the universe to himself, all that
is on earth and all that is in heaven, when he made peace
through his blood, shed on the cross. Your own hearts
were once hostile and estranged from God through your
misdeeds; but now God has reconciled you to himself
through Christ's death in his body of flesh, in order to
make you holy in his sight, free from blemish and free
from guilt.   (*Col 1:19-22*)

God is like that!

If any of you has a hundred sheep and loses one of them,
does he not leave the ninety-nine in the desert and go
after the lost sheep until he finds it? And when he finds
it, does he not put it on his shoulders joyfully, and come
home and call his friends and neighbours together and
say to them: 'Rejoice with me, because I have found the
sheep I had lost'?   (*Lk 15:3-6*)

Reinstatement

So he arose and went to his father. But while he was still far off, his father saw him and was filled with pity for him, and ran and put his arms round his neck and kissed him. His son said to him: 'Father, I have sinned against heaven and before you; I no longer deserve to be called your son.' But the father said to his servants: 'Quick! Bring the richest robe and put it on him; put a ring on his finger and sandals on his feet; bring the fatted calf and kill it, and let us eat and make merry, because this son of mine was dead and has come back to life, he was lost and now he is found.'   (*Lk 15:20-24*)

Reflection

St Paul's usual word for describing what happens to us through faith and baptism is 'justification'. But sometimes, as here in Colossians, he prefers to speak of 're-conciliation', which in many ways is a better word. We were estranged from God by our sins, says St Paul; but he has reconciled us to himself through Christ's death on the cross. In statements about our reconciliation, 'God' is always the subject: it is he who takes the initiative and reconciles us to himself. He goes out to look for the lost sheep; his holy Spirit is at work in the prodigal son before he rises and returns.

There can be few people who pass through this life without some fairly deep experience of estrangement and reconciliation. Estrangement from someone whom we love, perhaps within our own family, carries with it a sadness of its own; and reconciliation too is a deeply personal experience. Whereas 'justification' sounds judicial, objective and impersonal, reconciliation is possible only where there was and ought to be a bond of love. It is helpful to think of our relationship to God with the aid of this less judicial comparison. Personal relationships of all kinds are delicate; they are easily damaged, and far less easily repaired. If two men who are friends have a disagreement one day, and one bursts into a violent temper, the bond of reverence is damaged, and, in spite of much good will, may not be quite the same afterwards — unless perhaps the two go through some great trial and suffering together, in which case a new relationship can arise, not the same as before, but better (cf. Rom 5:17).

God created man to live at peace with him — to be the recipient of his love (what other reason had God for creating, but to give?). But the bond was broken by sin; death came into the world, and weakness; sin multiplied, and the estrangement grew. Men turned away from God because their deeds were evil; they withdrew into an unhappy and restless state of estrangement, which they could not fully understand, or remedy in any way.

But God did not change; his mercy endures for ever. In his Fatherly love he looked with sorrow on man's unhappiness; and being all-powerful he was able to repair the damage — and not just by words. First of all in deeds he showed his desire for reconciliation: he sent his Son to become a man and lead his brethren back to receive divine forgiveness, the kiss of peace, and the robe of sonship. At Christmas, the Child in the crib is often shown with his arms outstretched, appealing. Good three-dimensional theology! This was the purpose of Christ's life from the start — an offer of reconciliation.

Reconciliation is not achieved by words alone, but by doing and by suffering. God in his eternity was unable to suffer, but he sent his Son to take the form of man, so that in his human body he could himself bear the cost of our reconciliation. For thirty years he said nothing, and then he achieved his Father's saving will chiefly through suffering and death.

This is the good news of the gospel — sad good news, in a way — that God has reconciled us to himself through the death of his Son — sad, and yet at the same time deeply consoling to those who believe. To most men, alas, it is still too good to believe — that God grieves over our estrangement and has gone to such lengths to provide a remedy. Often we do not quite believe it ourselves; and if we do not watch, we can sink back insensibly into a certain estrangement, nursing a secret and almost unconscious grudge against God — as if the plans of his Fatherly providence were not quite good enough. So we turn away and wander in the darkness, as it were of a forest. But we know where the clearing is. We have only to turn back, away from the darkness, and knock on the door of our Father's house: 'Father, renew in me your Holy Spirit, the spirit of love, of joy, of peace.' Then he will take us into the warmth and light of his love. Reconciliation is a deep and tender experience, too deep for words, or even for actions. There are times when God can be addressed only in silence, or, as St Paul says, 'with sighs too deep for words.'

Prayer

Eternal Father, God of peace, we thank you for the reconciliation you have granted us through the death of your Son; and we pray that we may enter more deeply into the love and peace of your presence. Not for a fish do we ask, and not for an egg; but consume our hearts with the Spirit of your Son and the fire of his love.

8

The Sufferings
of Christ and of Paul

Filling up What is Wanting

You must remain firm and steadfast in your faith, immovably attached to the hope held out to you by the gospel which you have heard — the gospel that has been proclaimed to the whole creation under heaven, the gospel of which I, Paul, am a minister. At present I am suffering for your sake, and I am glad of it. I am helping to pay off in my person, on behalf of his body which is the Church, that which is wanting to Christ's afflictions. I have been appointed minister of this Church, in virtue of the office assigned me by God for your benefit, to make fully known the word of God.   (*Col 1:23-25*)

Servant and Master

If the world hates you, remember that it hated me before it hated you. If you were of the world, the world would love you as its own; but you are not of the world, because

I have chosen you out of the world, and therefore you are hated by the world. Remember my saying, 'The servant is not greater than his lord.' Have they persecuted me? They will persecute you. Have they heeded my word? No more will they heed yours. They will treat you in this way on account of my name, because they do not know the One who sent me.   *(Jn 15:18-21)*

Reflection

When St Paul was writing to the Philippians, he felt it necessary to explain how his imprisonment fitted into God's plans. [1] He said: 'Far from impeding the spread of the gospel, my imprisonment has proved a positive help — inside and outside the fortress, the gospel is being preached more openly.' When writing to the Colossians, he is again in prison, or still in prison, [2] and here too he feels that he must offer an explanation of his sufferings. This time, the explanation is different and deeper. He says: 'Part of my apostolic ministry is to suffer, and I am now suffering *on your behalf*' — a statement which may have come as a surprise to the Colossians. They knew that Christ had suffered on their behalf, but how could Paul say that he too was suffering on their behalf? And how could he dare to add that he was filling up in his body what was wanting to the sufferings of Christ? Did he mean that Christ's sufferings and merits were insufficient, and needed to be completed by his own? Surely not! But what then did he mean?

St Paul is not a systematic theologian. He says first that God has reconciled these Colossians to himself by the death of Christ; and then he adds that he himself is suffering for them to make up what is wanting —

---

[1] Cf. *Scripture for Meditation 2: Philippians,* pp. 23-24.
[2] On the problem of dating these Epistles, see *Philippians,* pp. 122-23

and he does not stop to explain how the second statement is to be harmonized with the first in a tidy theological system. He left quite a lot of tidying up to be done by others. Can we perhaps supply an explanation?

In St Thomas Aquinas's hymn *Adoro te devote*, there is a line which says that one drop of Christ's blood could have saved the whole world from all its sins. A striking thought! But one must add: Yes, it could have, *if God the Father had so willed*. But he did not so will. He willed that Christ should shed his blood in profusion; and he also willed that the body which is the Church should suffer along with its head, which is Christ. It was not his will that the head should suffer and the members should go scot free. In the gospel, Christ accordingly calls upon his disciples to share in his sufferings — to take up their cross and follow him. The Suffering Servant of Isaiah 53 is both an individual and a collective personality — Christ as the Head and Christ as the whole body.

We can look upon the plan of our redemption in this way: God sent his Son to call men to repentance and to set an *example* of penance by voluntary acceptance of suffering. In setting this example, Christ offered a *sacrifice* of expiation, not for his own sins (for he was sinless), but for the sins of others. His death was, therefore, both a sacrifice and an example. We must not so emphasize the sacrificial aspect of it that we forget that it was also an example. We too are called upon to take up our cross — to accept willingly the sufferings which God sends in our lives and offer them as a token of repentance, not for our own sins alone, but for the sins of others too. From Matthew 18 and other texts it is clear that the sins of any Christian are the concern and the burden of the whole Church. When we say 'Forgive us our trespasses', we are not praying each for himself alone, but each for all.

These reflections lead on to the further question: Why, if God could have saved us by the blood of his Son alone, did he will that something should be left over to be filled up by Paul, and by us? The answer may perhaps be that a perfect reconciliation is not possible without a sharing of suffering.

For a Christian, suffering should never be meaningless, and never wasted. As St Paul says at the end of the Epistle to the Galatians: 'Bear one another's burdens, and so you will fulfil the law of Christ.' When Christ bore the burden of the Cross, he was fulfilling his own law — bearing the burden of the sins of others. May we have the courage to follow him!

Prayer

Heavenly Father, who sent your Son to bear the burden of other men's sins, grant us the courage to share his burden, by carrying whatever cross you may lay upon our shoulders; and prevent us by your grace from increasing the burdens of others by neglecting your precept of love.

9

The Open Secret
of the Gospel

God's Plans Revealed at Last

At present I am suffering for your sake, and I am glad
of it. I am helping to pay off in my person, on behalf
of his body which is the Church, that which is wanting
to Christ's afflictions. I have been appointed minister of
this Church, in virtue of the office assigned me by God
for your benefit, to make fully known the word of God,
the mystery that was hidden through the ages and the
generations, but is now revealed to God's people. To
them God has been pleased to make known the generosity
of his glorious design among the Gentiles, namely, that
Christ is in your midst and is your hope of glory. He is
the one whom we preach. We admonish all mankind,
and instruct all mankind in all wisdom, so as to lead all
mankind to maturity in Christ. That is the end for which
I labour and strive, through the strength of him who
works in me with power.   (*Col 1:24-29*)

Words of Warning and Encouragement

Blessed are those who suffer persecution for the sake of justice, for theirs is the kingdom of heaven. Count yourselves blessed when you are insulted and persecuted and calumniated in every way because of me. Be glad of it, and rejoice in the thought that you will have a great reward in heaven. The prophets who went before you were persecuted in just this way.

You are the salt of the earth. (But if the salt loses its taste, what will you use to restore its saltiness? It is no longer good for anything except to be thrown out and trampled under men's feet.) You are the light of the world. A city built on a mountain-top cannot but be seen. When a lamp is lit, it is not put under a barrel but on a lampstand; then it gives light to everyone in the house. You too, in the same way, must let your light shine out before men, so that they will see your good works and give glory to your Father in heaven.

(Mt 5:10-16)

Reflection

This section of the Epistle enables us to look into St Paul's mind and see how he understood himself and his mission. He sees himself as one who has been chosen out to receive a precious and astounding revelation of the plans of God's providence, and to make this revelation known to all mankind. From the beginning of time, God has been patiently following out his plans for mankind, but in the past he kept them secret, or gave partial revelations — glimpses — to the patriarchs and prophets, to Abraham and to Isaiah. But now at last he has made known the whole plan to the apostles, and chiefly to Paul himself. Paul felt, without pride or humility, simply as a fact, that he had been enabled to understand better

than the others what he calls 'the glorious mystery' of
the faith: that Christ is not just the Messiah of the Jews
(though that alone would be something great) but is also
the Lord of all the Gentiles, and is already at work
among the Gentiles, creating a new people of God, fulfilling in a marvellous way the ancient promise to Abraham. To us, this idea is so familiar that it no longer
causes wonder; but to Paul, a Hebrew of the Hebrews,
it was *the* great 'mystery' of the faith — that salvation
is offered to Jew and Gentile alike on the same terms
of faith in Christ, and that it is the Gentiles who are
accepting the offer!

When St Paul calls this a 'mystery', he does not
mean that it is mysterious and hard to understand. It is
not, the idea is very simple. What he means is that this
is the fulfilment of a wonderful plan which God kept
secret through the ages, and has now at last revealed to
Paul and through Paul to all men. The mystery is now
a 'revealed mystery' or an open secret to all who believe.

St Paul realizes, then, that to himself has fallen a
truly cardinal role in the history of salvation — that is
to say, a pivotal role, so much turns upon him. I was
once talking to a learned Jew who made the remarkable
pun that 'But for Paul, Christianity would have petered
out in the second century.' This would have been a
little hard on Peter, if the pun had been deliberate; but
the observation was sound in so far as Paul was the
apostle who, in God's providence, planted the faith se-
curely in the Gentile world, so that when Jewish Christianity was almost extinguished in the upheavals of the
years 66 to 70, the Church survived and flourished in
the Gentile world. Paul rightly believed that he was
fulfilling a pivotal role, and he did not hesitate to say so
— though he was careful to add that he fulfilled this
office by the strength of Christ who worked in him with
power.

As the passage from St Matthew shows, Christ meant the apostles to be conscious of their dignity: 'You are the salt of the earth....you are the light of the world.' These are intoxicating words which might go to a man's head, but they are true: without knowledge of God's plans for them, men will wander in darkness, and their lives will be corrupted by ignorance and sin. The truth of the gospel is the salt that will preserve them from corruption, and the light that will make their lives meaningful.

Men, women, and children *need* this knowledge. Without it they are living in an unintelligible world; with it, they can understand and cooperate with God's plans. As St Paul says here, mankind cannot come to maturity without this knowledge. If a man is to become a spiritual adult, he must understand the world, God's plans for the world, and his own place in these plans. The task of an apostle, ancient or modern, is to help men and women to a correct self-understanding. Each individual who comes into the world finds himself, the world, God, other people — and must learn how these are related to one another, and how he himself can become a meaningful part of this great whole. The knowledge is not innate. The gospel is God's answer to these questions, the true answer; and without the true answer neither the individual man, nor mankind as a whole, can attain maturity.

Recall what St Paul was saying earlier in the Epistle about the primacy of Christ in the order of creation and in the order of redemption. This means that Christ created man and set him in this world, as we might plant a young tree, intending that it should grow to maturity. But the development of man was stunted and spoiled by sin. So Christ came in the likeness of man to provide the remedy. The man who accepts the revelation offered him in the gospel and cooperates with it, has the remedy, and will grow to the maturity which Christ intended from the beginning — or perhaps to an even greater perfection, since where sin abounded grace has more than abounded.

All of us who share in the apostolic vocation in our various ways, should reflect what a high privilege it is to cooperate with Christ in this way, what responsibilities this privilege carries with it, and what happens to the salt that loses its taste. We should also reflect how urgently our fellow men *need* this revelation, even if through the darkness of sin they think they have no need of it. They may insult us, and sometimes do, but we must love those who hate us and overcome evil with good.

Prayer

Heavenly Father, who called us to share in the work of spreading the gospel, grant that we may rightly value the honour we have received and worthily discharge our office. Give us a deeper understanding of the teaching of our Divine Master, and be with us always, as we seek to teach it by example.

D

10

True Wisdom

Seek Wisdom!

My son, if you receive my words
    and treasure up my commandments with you,
making your ear attentive to wisdom
    and inclining your heart to understanding;
yes, if you cry out for insight
    and raise your voice for understanding,
if you seek it like silver
    and search for it as for hidden treasures,
then you will understand the fear of the Lord
    and find the knowledge of God.
For the Lord gives wisdom;
    from his mouth come knowledge and understanding.
                            (Prov 2:1-6)

Wisdom commends Herself

Come to me, you who desire me,
    and eat your fill of my produce.
For the remembrance of me is sweeter than honey,
    and my inheritance sweeter than the honeycomb.

Those who eat me will hunger for more,
    and those who drink me will thirst for more.
Whoever obeys me will not be put to shame,
    and those who work with my help will not sin.
(Sirach 24:19-22)

Christ offers Wisdom

I thank you, Father, Lord of heaven and earth, because while concealing these things from the wise and prudent, you have revealed them to the simple; yes Father, I thank you, because this has been your good pleasure.

Everything has been delivered to me by my Father, and no one knows the Son except the Father, nor does anyone know the Father except the Son, and those to whom the Son chooses to reveal him.

Come to me, all who are weary and overburdened, and I will give you rest; for I am meek and humble of heart. Take my yoke upon you and learn from me, and you will find rest for your souls; for my yoke is easy and the burden light. *(Mt 11:25-30)*

The Treasury of Wisdom

I want you to know how great a contest I am undergoing — for your sake, for those at Laodicea, and for all others who have not seen me in person, that their hearts may take courage, that they may be united in charity and enriched with perfect understanding, and so attain to full knowledge of God's mystery — that is, to full knowledge of Christ, in whom all the treasures of wisdom and knowledge are concealed. I say this, so that no one will mislead you with persuasive talk. Although I am absent in body, I am with you in spirit, and I rejoice to see your good order and the firmness of your faith in Christ.
(Col 2:1-5)

Reflection

St Paul is in prison, suffering for Christ, and is glad to do so, because such is the will of God. But if it were the will of God that he should visit the Colossians and other new communities of Gentile Christians, he would be equally glad, or more so. Since he cannot be physically present, he wants to be at least spiritually present to them — and them to him. He wants them to know what he is suffering for the sake of the gospel and what prayers he is making for them in the midst of his sufferings, so that they will be encouraged by the knowledge that he is offering prayer and penance for them, and will be emboldened by his example to suffer something for the sake of the true gospel.

The substance of his prayer is that the Colossians may fully grasp the truth: that the wisdom which Christ possesses and offers to his disciples is superior to any other. Man is not born wise; he lacks the knowledge (in Greek the *gnôsis*) which he needs in order to live in peace and harmony with his fellow men. Therefore he is commanded, both by his conscience and by the Scriptures, to seek wisdom from those who have it — from prophets and wise men. God gives his gifts of prophecy and moral insight to a few prophetic figures for the guidance of the rest. As the Greek poet Hesiod observed, in the time of Amos and Micah, 'that man is best who is able to discern all things for himself; next best is he who learns from the wise; but he who neither discovers for himself nor heeds another is an utterly worthless fellow.'

The Jews were encouraged by their own Wisdom-literature to believe that all wisdom was already available to them in the Torah. In chapter 24 of the Wisdom of Ben Sirach, the strange female personification of Wisdom (*Sophia*) offers her gift of wisdom to the Jews and suddenly announces that this wisdom *is* the law which Moses gave. Ben Sirach meant that the Greek-speaking Jews for whom he wrote were to seek wisdom, not from the Greek philosophers, but from their own tradition, starting from Moses. Naturally, therefore, the Jew believed that he had in the law of Moses 'the perfect pattern of knowledge (*gnôsis*) and of truth' and was thereby equipped to be 'guide to the blind, a light for those in darkness, an educator of the foolish, and a teacher of little ones' (cf. Rom 2: 19-20).

When Jesus appeared among the Jews, he placed himself in contrast to the Mosaic tradition and above it: 'It was said to those of old....but I say to you...' As the unique Son of God, he possessed knowledge of God's will which surpassed the wisdom embodied in the law. Echoing the language of Wisdom, he speaks as the True Wisdom when he offers his easy yoke. Thus the gospel proclaims that wisdom will be found by those who seek it, neither from the Greek philosophers, nor from the Jewish law, but from the mouth of Christ. 'Hear *him!*' said the voice at the Transfiguration. He is the world's Teacher. He points out the way of justice which leads to life and more abundant life.

St Paul repeats this message for the Colossians. They must accept no inferior substitute which offers itself as wisdom or knowledge (*gnôsis*). The treasures of wisdom and knowledge are hidden in the breast of Christ, who reveals them as he wills to whom he wills.

Prayer

O Lord Jesus Christ, in whom are all the treasures of wisdom and knowledge, we entrust ourselves to your teaching without reserve; place your easy yoke upon us, and help us to bear it willingly and gladly, for the glory of God our Father.

11

False Wisdom

Christian Pharisaism

Some teachers came down from Judaea (to Antioch) and
began saying to the brethren: 'Unless you are circumcised and live according to the custom of Moses, you
cannot be saved.' Paul and Barnabas vigorously opposed
them and argued against them, but in the end it was
decided to send Paul and Barnabas and some others
from Antioch to put this problem before the apostles
and presbyters in Jerusalem. They were set on their way
by the church, and went through Phoenicia and Samaria,
where they reported the conversion of the Gentiles and
brought great joy to all the brethren. When they arrived
in Jerusalem, they were welcomed by the church and by
the apostles and presbyters, and reported to them all that
God had enabled them to do. But some who had been
converted to the faith from the sect of the Pharisees rose
up and said: 'The Gentiles must be circumcised and
told to keep the law of Moses.'   (*Acts 15:1-5*)

Expostulation to the Galatians

Formerly, not knowing God, you were the slaves of beings who by nature are not gods; but now that you have come to know God, or rather to be known by God, how can you turn back to the weak and grasping elements? Do you wish to be enslaved to them all over again, observing days and months and seasons and years? I fear I may have laboured in vain for you.   (*Gal 4:8-11*)

Warning to the Colossians

Since the message delivered to you was that Christ Jesus is Lord, live your lives in union with him, rooted in him, founded on him. Hold fast to the faith in the form in which you were taught it, and be abundantly grateful for it. Watch that no one captivates you with philosophy and empty deceit — with a man-made wisdom which would subject you to the elemental powers of the world and not to Christ. For the fulness of the Godhead dwells in his body, and in union with him you lack nothing. He is the head of every power and principality. In him you have received a spiritual circumcision, not a surgical operation for the removal of bodily flesh, but Christ's circumcision.   (*Col 2:6-11*)

Reflection

St Paul's purpose in emphasizing that Christ is the source of all true wisdom is to forearm the Colossians against a type of religious propaganda which he describes as 'philosophy and empty deceit'. The meaning or reference of this deliberately pejorative description is much debated. The question is often put in the form: What was the exact nature of the Colossian heresy? Some highly complicated answers have been given: that the Colossians had fused together into a syncretistic system elements of Greek philosophy, Christianity, unorthodox Judaism and Iranian Gnosticism. [1] Learned conjectures of this kind have a depressing effect. We are made to feel that, as the error which St Paul is attacking is beyond our comprehension, we cannot hope to learn much from the Epistle. Let me propose a much simpler answer which has the double advantage of being far less depressing and probably correct.

It seems most unlikely that the newly-founded church of Colossae, numbering perhaps fifty members, had already elaborated an heretical syncretism of its own. In his opening prayer St Paul prayed, encouragingly, that they would persevere in the teaching which they had received from his disciple Epaphras. At the corresponding point in the Epistle to the Galatians (1:6), he adopts an entirely different tone: 'I am astonished that you are so quickly abandoning the gospel!' St Paul shows no sign of anger with the Colossians; he does not accuse them of departing from the gospel, nor does he anathemize anyone for upsetting them (contrast Gal 1:8-9). Probably the church of Colossae is still at peace; it has not yet been invaded by the false doctrines which St Paul has in mind. He wants to put them on their guard, in preparation for the day when its exponents will come to tempt them.

What, then, is the false doctrine which he has in mind? The simplest answer is probably the correct one: it is the same error which upset the Galatian churches

---

[1] 'Gnosticism' is an ill-defined term, which rarely adds clarity to any discussion. If any religion which makes salvation depend on 'knowledge' is Gnostic, Christianity is a Gnostic religion. But the word is usually restricted to dualistic systems, which picture the universe as a battlefield of good and evil, both irreducibles.

about the same time, or a few years earlier. [1] The
teachers who propagate it are Pharisees converted to
Christianity, like those who upset the church of Antioch
and later the churches of Galatia. Their principal doctrines were: first, that Gentile converts must 'judaize',
that is, must submit to circumcision and obey the law
of Moses; secondly, that as the law was given to Moses
by angels, these angels must be held in veneration; and
thirdly, that if a Christian will impose upon himself
severe fasts, he will probably see visions of angels who
will give him secret 'knowledge' (*gnôsis*) or private revelations (perhaps like those described in the Apocalypse).

St Paul forearms the Colossians against this man-
made system of religion (which is more Jewish than
Christian) by answering its three principal points: first,
he says, circumcision is only a material symbol of death
— a token stripping-away of the body, but we have the
spiritual reality: in baptism we die and rise with Christ.
Therefore we have no need of physical circumcision.
Secondly, St Paul agrees that the law of Moses was
given by angels. [2] But, he adds, one mark of the su-
periority of Christianity over Judaism is that in Christ
God has taken bodily form and deals directly with man;
he no longer uses angels as intermediaries. Veneration
of the angels of the law is, therefore, at best an ana-
chronism. Thirdly, St Paul says, no one should place
his trust in alleged visions of angels. These angels, whom
he describes as 'elemental (or elementary) powers', are
themselves only creatures of Christ. The wisdom and
knowledge of Christ who created them is infinitely superior to their elementary wisdom. Indeed, Christ, being

---

[1] If Colossians was written from Ephesus during the third
missionary journey, the two Epistles cannot be separated by
much more than two years.

[2] Cf. Gal 3 : 19. St Stephen too accepted this opinion; cf. Acts
7 : 38,53.

God, possesses locked up in his breast all the treasures of wisdom and knowledge that belong to the Godhead. Therefore the Colossians must hold fast to their faith in Christ and refuse to be distracted by specious promises of angelic revelations.

When St Paul says that the treasures of wisdom and knowledge are *concealed* in Christ, he may mean that though they are destined to remain concealed, they make Christ the perfect Lord and Master, to whom we can entrust our lives without reservation. He is far more worthy of trust than angels who possess only a partial understanding of God's plans, or human teachers who claim to have received private revelations from angels. But St Paul may also mean that the treasures of wisdom, though now concealed, are destined to be revealed to those who believe. Prophecy was still common in the pauline churches, and Paul himself had an abundance of visions (cf. 2 Cor 12:7). The true *gnôsis* is Christ's gift, and it is a matter of being known rather than of knowing. We do not embrace God; he embraces us and communicates his life to us.

Prayer

To you, Lord Jesus, I entrust my life, for I believe that you possess all wisdom and knowledge and are willing to be my Master and Guide. Impart to me the wisdom I need for myself and my fellow men, and give me faith enough to follow you peacefully, even when I cannot fully understand your ways.

12

Christ in our Midst

The Mystery of Baptism

The fulness of the Godhead dwells in his body, and in
union with him you lack nothing. He is the fountain-head
of every power and principality. In him you have received a spiritual circumcision — not a surgical operation
for the removal of bodily flesh, but Christ's circumcision.
You have been buried with him through your faith in
the power of God who raised him from the dead. You too
were once dead, because of your sins and because your
natural being was uncircumcised; but God has restored
you to life with Christ.   (*Col 2:9-13*)

Faith and Resurrection

As soon as Jesus crossed back in the boat to the other
side, a great crowd gathered to meet him. He was still
on the shore, when a president of one of the synagogues
came to him. Jairus was his name. He fell at Jesus' feet

when he saw him, and earnestly begged his help: 'My little daughter is at the point of death,' he said, 'come and lay your hands on her, and save her life.' So Jesus went away with him, accompanied by great crowds which pressed about him.

There was a woman who had suffered from haemorrhages for twelve years, and had endured much at the hands of many doctors, and spent all she had without becoming any the better but rather worse. As she had heard about Jesus, she came up behind him in the crowd and touched his cloak, thinking to herself: 'If I touch even his clothes I shall be healed.' At once the source of the haemorrhages was dried up, and she felt in her body that she was cured of her complaint. Jesus knew at once that power had gone out from him, and he turned round in the crowd and said: 'Who touched my clothes?' His disciples said: 'With the crowds as you see pressing round you, how can you ask, "Who touched me?"' Jesus was looking round to see who had done it. But the woman, who was in fear and trembling because she knew what had happened to her, came and fell at his feet and told him the whole truth. He said to her: 'Daughter, your faith has cured you. Go in peace, and you will remain free from your complaint.'

While he was still speaking, a message came from the house of the president of the synagogue: 'Your daughter is dead; why trouble the Master further?' But Jesus overheard the message and said to the president: 'Do not be downhearted; only have faith!' He allowed no one to accompany him except Peter and James, and John the brother of James. When they reached the president's house, he found a noisy crowd of people wailing and lamenting loudly. So, as he went in, he said to them: 'What is the reason for this noise and lamentation? The child is not dead; she is only asleep.' They laughed at him: but after he had sent them all away, he took the child's father and mother and his own companions, and went into the room where the child lay. He took her by the hand and said to her: '*Talitha, koum,*' which means: 'Little girl, (I bid you) rise up!' At once the girl rose up and began to walk about (she was twelve years old) and the people were beside themselves with amazement.

(*Mk 5:21-42*)

Reflection

It is part of the task of an apostle or preacher to help his hearers to attain a correct understanding of themselves and of the world in which God has put them. That is what St Paul is doing here. He is saying that the condition of men and women in the world has been radically changed by the coming of Christ: now God dwells in our midst — in the midst of the Gentiles — in human form. This means that a new source of power is available within the human family, to energize the hearts and minds of men and women. Before Christ came, this source of power was not there. The Jews had the law, but the law itself was not a source of life. To make the Jews aware of their sinfulness, the Lord laid down material rites of purification, such as circumcision and the levitical sacrifices; but these things were not in themselves effective of forgiveness; they were only symbols pointing forward to the future. During a debate with the Jews in Jerusalem, Jesus says to his opponents (Jn 5:39-40): 'You study the Scriptures, thinking that in them you have the source of eternal life — you study the very Scriptures that bear witness to me; and yet you will not come to me, to have that life!' Jesus *is* what the Jews thought the Torah was: the divine power and wisdom present on earth in bodily form.

Since he came to dwell in the midst of the nations, the situation of all men is different. A new source of power and life is available to all, free of cost, and those who plug into it by faith find themselves changed men. Christ does for them what the law could not do. The difference between the condition of men before and after belief in Christ is the difference between sleeping and waking, or between being dead and being risen. According to St Paul's doctrine of original sin, all men are born spiritually dead. They think they are well enough, but they are not — their spiritual vitality is at a very low ebb; but they are unaware of this, because they have never known anything different. To such people Paul proclaims that if they will now believe that in Christ risen from the dead the fulness of the Godhead is bodily present, and if they will appeal to him for strength, he will fill them with fresh vitality which they never had before, and they will feel that they too are risen from the dead. St Paul is here speaking from his own experience. Since his conversion and baptism, he has felt himself to be a new man, filled with a power from on high.

To the modern reader, all this may seem a trifle exaggerated. We have believed in Christ, probably from childhood, and do here and now believe in him; and yet quite frequently we feel more dead than alive — and at times, I suppose, we are all disgusted with our own mediocrity. Perhaps we can learn a lesson from this long passage of St Mark: both the incidents narrated in it show that Christ's power is available to those who believe in his power and who *want* to experience its effects. The raising of Jairus's daughter shows that his power is the power of resurrection — power to call the dead and the sleepers to life, even through the prayers of others. The cure of the woman with haemorrhages illustrates very well St Paul's saying earlier in the Epistle (1:27) that the mystery of God is 'Christ in your midst'. In the gospel scene, Christ is in the midst of a crowd, jostled on all sides, but only one woman profits by his touch and draws on his power. She is blessed above the rest, because she is aware of her need and believes in Christ's power to cure her. She knows that there is a wound deep in her nature, robbing her of strength and life, and that Christ alone can cure it. [1]

One reason why St Paul was so emphatically opposed to the introduction of Jewish ritual practices into the Gentile churches was that he could see the effect of such practices on the Jews: the ceremonial law lulled them into a false security and complacency. They said to themselves: 'We have circumcision, we observe the law, we are children of Abraham, we are God's chosen people. What more do we need?' In that frame of mind they could not recognize their need of Christ to be their Saviour.

The reason why we do not find Christ's power more active in the modern world may be that we, his latterday disciples, are too easily satisfied with our present condition. We do not recognize our own defects and weaknesses. Perhaps we have heard so much about sacramental confession of our sins that we forget the prior duty of interior confession to Christ in the secrecy of our hearts. In books and leaflets on examination of conscience we are usually told first to make an act of thanksgiving, secondly to pray for light to see our faults, thirdly to examine our consciences, and fourthly to make an act of contrition. But would it not be well to insert between the third and fourth points, a private confession of our sins and weaknesses to God in the secrecy of our hearts? Then, being aware of our own defects, we might pray more effectively for their cure.

---

[1] The evangelist who first combined this miracle with the resurrection of Jairus's daughter may well have seen in her malady a symbol of original sin.

Prayer

Lord Jesus, our Saviour, look with mercy on the sickness
of my spirit. My heart is proud and unforgiving....Touch
me with your grace and heal me both of these and of my
more hidden faults.

13

The Cross
and the Old Religion

The End of an Era

You too were once dead, because of your sins and because
your natural being was uncircumcised; but God has restored you to life with Christ by forgiving all your sins
— by cancelling the invoice of debts to the law which
stood against us, nailing it to the cross. He has disarmed
the powers and dominations and made a public spectacle
of them, leading them as prisoners in his triumph. Therefore let no one call you to account for what you eat or
drink, or for the observance of festivals, new moons or
sabbaths. These things were but the shadow of what was
to come; the reality is Christ. If anyone claims to have
had visions, and then with affected self-abasement advocates the worship of angels, he must not be allowed
to impose his will on you. Such a teacher is puffed out
with the futile conceits of his own natural mind; he has
not maintained union with the head from which the
whole body, through its joints and ligaments, is supplied
with nourishment, given solidity and made to fill out as

65

God would have it grow. If you have died with Christ
and escaped from subjection to the elements of the world,
why live as if you still belonged to the world? Why let
men make rules for you: 'Do not touch this! Do not
taste that! Do not handle the other!' — rules concerning
only material things which perish in the very use? Would
you follow human doctrines and precepts? They have
an appearance of wisdom, with their talk of 'voluntary
veneration', 'self-abasement', and 'corporal austerity'; but
they are of no true worth, and lead only to gratification
of the natural man. *(Col 2:13-23)*

Man-made Traditions

Some Pharisees and a number of scribes who had come
from Jerusalem gathered round Jesus. [1] They had seen
some of his disciples taking their meals with unwashed
hands, or as they say, with hands 'defiled'. (The Pharisees, and indeed all Jews, do not eat unless they have
first washed their hands to the elbow; in this they are
keeping to a tradition of their ancestors; and on coming
from the market place they do not eat until they have
sprinkled themselves with water. And there are many
other traditional practices which they hold as binding,
such as the washing of cups and bowls and pans.) So the
Pharisees and scribes asked him: 'Why do your disciples
abandon the traditions of their ancestors and take their
meals with hands defiled?' He answered: 'The prophet
Isaiah gave a good description of you hypocrites when
he said: "This people honours me with lip-service, but
their hearts are far away from me; the worship they pay
me is worthless, for the doctrines they teach are commandments made by man." You renounce God's law
and cling to human traditions.' *(Mk 7:1-8)*

---

[1] Cf. Acts 15:1, quoted above, p. 54.

The Cleansing of the Temple

When they came into Jerusalem, Jesus went into the temple and drove out those who were buying and selling there, and he overturned the tables of the money-changers and the benches of the dove-sellers. He would not allow anyone to carry any burden through the temple precincts. To explain what he had done, he said to them: 'Does not the Scripture say: "My house shall be called a house of prayer for all the nations"? But you have turned it into a den of thieves.' The chief priests and scribes heard of this, and they considered how they could make an end of him, because all the people were full of admiration for his teaching. *(Mk 11:15-18)*

Reflection

At the beginning of this section of the Epistle, there is a striking image to help us to appreciate what Christ did for us on the cross. Whenever the Romans crucified a man, they nailed up on his cross a title or inscription stating the crime for which he was being put to death. In the case of Christ our Lord, Pilate did the usual thing, but he mocked the Jews by simply putting up 'The King of the Jews'. The Jewish rulers asked him to correct it and write: 'He claimed to be the King of the Jews' — that was the charge on which he was condemned. St Paul here says: If you want to understand the cross, imagine Pilate's title removed, and instead — a list of your own sins stuck up there on the nail. That is what Christ is really dying for: to wipe out the list of crimes for which *you* ought otherwise to have suffered.

From there, St Paul passes on to an idea which is less familiar to us. Some of his contemporaries among the Jews believed, and St Paul seems to have agreed, that the law was not only given by angels, but also enforced by angels. They believed that God left the punishment of sinners to certain angels who were the ministers of his wrath. Out of reverence for the holiness and majesty of God, they held that he neither imposed sanctions nor enforced them. He himself gave to Israel only the ten commandments, which have the form of a father's advice to his sons and specify no sanction. On this view, if a man broke the laws added by angels through their human intermediaries, he incurred a debt of punishment to these angels, and so fell under their power. [1] It follows that when Christ on Calvary paid the bill for us, he was robbing these angels of their prey. As St Paul says, he disarmed them and made them powerless. Indeed he went further and put them in the wrong: their law says in Deuteronomy: 'Cursed is every man who hangs upon a tree.' When Christ died hanging on a tree, he came under their curse and put them in the wrong! It is of course a serious problem for us how far we can take over these elements in St Paul's thought; but at least we can follow his argument.

Look, he says, at the cross! There your sins were expiated and the angels of the law were discredited. Can you be so foolish as to turn away from the cross and back to the religious rites of those discredited angels and their misguided human minions? These Jewish teachers who want Gentile Christians to judaize are seeking to perpetuate an obsolete religion. They do not realize that those material rites were only a shadow and a symbol. We have the reality in the cross. What further need have we then of all their rules and regulations about eating and drinking, and feast days and fast days? Do you want to go on living like children from one holiday to the next? Those Jewish teachers sound impressive with their

---

[1] These views are explained at some length in the works of Philo. See *Galatians,* pp. 304-307.

long words and their complicated calendar of feast days, but there is no substance in it all; they seem big men, but they are puffed up with a wisdom created in their own brains. The true wisdom consists in recognizing that the cross renders all the old rituals obsolete: the man who clings to Christ through faith will draw strength and nourishment from him, and will fill out into a solid body. He will become a well-built adult, not just a blown up infant.

In the first of the two passages from St Mark, Jesus warns the Jews that the observance of man-made traditions is no substitute for true religion. When Jesus went into the temple, he found the Jews busily buying and selling and changing money from one currency to another. These things were not religion, though done under the cloak of religion. They were a counterfeit; and, as is well known, if a counterfeit is not suppressed, it will infallibly drive out the true coinage. The religion of material rites and practices had to be suppressed in order to make room for worship in spirit and truth. In chapter 3 of the Epistle, St Paul will explain in some detail what God does require of Gentile Christians.

Prayer

Through the gift of your Spirit, O heavenly Father, let that mind be in us which was in Jesus Christ your Son, when he offered himself a faultless victim to you and put an end to the religious childhood of mankind. Teach us to worship you in spirit and truth, trusting in your Fatherly Providence, bearing with one another, and serving one another in charity.

14

Who knows God?

Elijah at Horeb

Elijah went a day's journey into the wilderness, and came and sat down under a broom tree; and he asked that he might die, saying: 'It is enough; now, O Lord, take away my life; for I am no better than my fathers.' And he lay down and slept under a broom tree; and behold, an angel touched him, and said to him: 'Arise and eat.' And he looked, and behold, there was at his head a cake baked on hot stones and a jar of water. And he ate and drank, and lay down again. And the angel of the Lord came a second time, and touched him, and said: 'Arise and eat, else the journey will be too great for you.' And he arose, and ate and drank, and went in the strength of that food forty days and forty nights to Horeb the mount of God.

And there he came to a cave, and lodged there; and behold, the word of the Lord came to him and he said to him: ....'Go forth and stand upon the mount before the Lord.' And behold, the Lord passed by, and a great and strong wind rent the mountains, and broke in pieces the rocks before the Lord, but the Lord was not in the wind; and after the wind an earthquake, but the Lord was not in the earthquake; and after the earthquake a fire, but the Lord was not in the fire, and after the fire a still small voice. *(1 Kgs 19:4-9,11-12)*

Visionary Religion

Let no one call you to account for what you eat or drink, or for the observance of festivals, new moons or sabbaths. These things were but the shadow of what was to come; the reality is Christ. If anyone claims to have had visions, and then with affected self-abasement advocates the worship of angels, he must not be allowed to impose his will on you. Such a teacher is puffed up with the futile conceits of his own natural mind; he has not maintained union with the head from which the whole body, through its joints and ligaments, is supplied with nourishment, given solidity and made to fill out as God would have it grow. If you have died with Christ and escaped from subjection to the elements of the world, why live as if you still belonged to the world? Why let men make rules for you: 'Do not touch this! Do not taste that! Do not handle the other!' — rules concerning only material things which perish in the very use? Would you follow human doctrines and precepts? They have an appearance of wisdom, with their talk of 'voluntary veneration', 'self-abasement', and 'corporal austerity'; but they are of no true worth, and lead only to gratification of the natural man. *(Col 2:16-23)*

The True Gnosis

My dear children, I am writing you this to keep you from sin. But if any of us does commit a sin, we have an Advocate before the Father, Jesus Christ, the Just

One. He is the expiation of our sins, and not of ours only, but of the sins of all the world.

We may find out whether we know him by this test: Do we keep his commandments? Anyone who claims to 'know' him, and yet does not keep his commandments, is a liar, and the truth is not in him; but whoever does keep his word — truly in him the love of God has reached its perfection; for that is the sign by which we know that we are in him. The man who claims to 'abide in him' must walk the same path as Christ walked.

(*1 Jn 2:1-6*)

Reflection

It is natural enough for a man to long to see the God who made him. Plato dreamed of a philosophical ascent towards contemplation of the source of all goodness; and platonizing Christians have always shared his aspiration after a mystical, visionary ascent to God even in this life. Mediaeval theologians of the Victorine and Franciscan schools loved to map out the soul's itinerary to God through successive grades of spiritual contemplation.

The Jewish teachers whose doctrine St Paul repudiates may have been influenced by the Greek philosophers (to whom Philo is deeply indebted). But they could also find in their own Biblical tradition suggestions of a mystical, visionary, or 'Gnostic' approach towards God. Elijah, for example, fasts for forty days and is given a 'vision' of God by an angel at Horeb (i.e., Sinai). Might not, then, a Christian Jew hope that if he practised a severe fast and implored the aid of angels, he too would be granted access to God through a vision? It seems that some of the Pharisaic teachers had followed this way, had seen visions, and were proud of it. The experience of some mediaeval saints and more recently of prisoners in concentration camps shows that prolonged fasting does induce visionary or hallucinatory experiences.

St Paul warns the Colossians against seeking this kind of 'knowledge' of God. So too does St John in his first Epistle. The test, he says, of whether a man 'knows' God is not whether he has seen any visions, but whether he keeps the commandments. To 'know' God is to experience the influence of his goodness and power. They manifest themselves in a man's conduct. That is why 'knowing' God is more a matter of being known than of active knowing (cf. Gal 4:9). A Christian who prides himself on visions, induced by fasting, but does not keep the commandments, is most probably deluded.

In this life, we are called upon to live by faith, not by vision. If we maintain contact with Christ through faith, he will supply us with energy from above and we shall grow in spiritual stature by fulfilling God's commands. He may or may not reveal to us the treasures of wisdom that are hidden in his breast; but if we obey his teaching with trust in his assistance, we shall learn in the toils and sufferings of our daily lives, who he is in whom we have trusted. [1]

Prayer

Heavenly Father, may I one day see your face! So long as it is your will that I should live by faith, give me a strong faith overflowing into works of charity. And in the midst of these let me experience your divine companionship.

---

[1] Cf. A. Schweitzer, *The Quest of the Historical Jesus*, London, 1910, p. 403.

15

Christian
Otherworldliness

Citizens of another World

If you have died with Christ and escaped from subjection
to the elements of the world, why live as if you still belonged to the world? Why let men make rules for you:
'Do not touch this! Do not taste that! Do not handle
the other!' — rules concerning only material things
which perish in the very use?....If you have risen with
Christ, seek the things that are above, where Christ is
seated at God's right hand. Set your thoughts on heavenly
things, not on the things of earth. For you are dead!
And your life is hidden with Christ in God.

(Col 2:20—3:3)

Lift up your eyes!

Do not be anxious about what you eat or drink for the
support of your life, nor about what clothes you wear
for the good of your body: is not your life something
greater than its food, and your body something greater

than its clothing? Look at the birds of the air: they do not sow or reap or gather into barns, yet your heavenly Father looks after them. Are you not much more valuable than they are? And which of you, by putting his mind to it, could add eighteen inches to his height? Why are you anxious about your clothes? Look at the lilies of the field and how they grow: they do not labour, they do not spin; and yet I tell you, not even Solomon in all his glory was dressed as splendidly as one of these! If then God clothes in this way the grass of the field, which lives today and tomorrow is thrown into the oven, will he not do even more for you, men of little faith? Then do not ask, 'What are we going to eat?' or 'What are we going to drink?' or 'What are we going to wear?' Those are the things the Gentiles are bent upon. Do not be anxious, for your heavenly Father is aware that you need all these things. Seek first the kingdom of God and his justice; then all these things will be given to you in addition.

(Mt 6:25-33)

Reflection

Earlier in the Epistle, St Paul has already shown that from the religious point of view, history is not homogeneous. During the interim-period from Moses to Christ, the Jews were made subject to the angels of the law, who imposed material rituals concerned with eating, drinking, washing, wearing phylacteries and fringes, and so on — things which were only shadows and symbols of future realities. Since the coming of Christ, the reign of the angelic powers, and the elementary rules which they impose, have been obsolete; a new power is at work in the world, and the condition of men and women has been different.

In the present section of the Epistle, St Paul adds that the new period inaugurated by Christ's death and resurrection is again only an interim. We have died with

Christ out of the old aeon where the angels reign, and have risen with him into a new era where Christ alone reigns at the right hand of the Father. We have died and have risen, *but we have not yet been glorified,* at least not visibly.

In this respect we resemble Christ our Lord: he died and has risen. He is also glorified, but not in the eyes of men. His glory is hidden 'in God'. It is concealed from men and revealed only to God and his heavenly court. So too with us, St Paul says: we have died and risen with Christ, and in the eyes of God we are glorified — because the glorious life of Christ is already at work within us. Our glory is hidden from all men's eyes, including our own. But when the glory of Christ is revealed at his Coming, the glory hidden within us too will be revealed, as part of the glory of Christ. Our own state of being, since our baptism, is much more mysterious and more wonderful than perhaps we realize. In the eyes of God all his children glow with a halo of the glory of Christ; his glory is mirrored on our brows (cf. 2 Cor 3:18). The old-fashioned pictures of saints with haloes were not entirely wrong. Already we are citizens of the heavenly kingdom — and already we are like Christ in being the bearers of a secret wisdom. Of his fulness we have received a share, while the unbelieving world remains in darkness.

These things being so, the Colossians should beware of teachers who tell them that religion consists in observing certain rules about what they eat, what they drink, and what they put on. These things belong to the elementary religion of the elemental powers. Christians must lift their thoughts higher, to the heavenly kingdom where Christ reigns. We must worship God by imitating Christ, his visible Image.

In the passage from the Sermon on the Mount, Jesus is not attacking ritual law. He is exhorting poor people not to be anxious about material things, to leave them to God's providence, and seek God's kingdom and its justice. St Paul sees that imposing a ritual law is another way of tying men's minds down to material things, instead of liberating them to seek the things that are above. The Pharisee in our Lord's parable talks to God about food and drink and money. The publican, though he does not raise his eyes to heaven, lifts up his heart in a petition for the spiritual gift of forgiveness.

Prayer

O heavenly Father, strengthen my belief in your presence within me, and lift up my soul with the power of your Spirit; inspire me to pray for what you want to give, and always to be grateful for what I have received.

16

Christian Asceticism

Be what you are!

The day will come when Christ, who is our life, will be
revealed; then you too will be revealed with him in glory.
Therefore make your bodies dead to earthly passions:
have done with fornication, impurity, lust, evil desires,
and that greed for money which is a form of idolatry.
Those are the things which bring down God's anger.
You yourselves once walked that way, when you lived
that kind of life. But now you must strip yourselves of
every vice, of anger, passion and baseness; cleanse your
lips of profane and vulgar speech; and do not tell lies
to one another. Put off your old selves and your evil
ways, and put on the new man, the nature that is being
restored in the image of its Creator and brought to know
him better.   (*Col 3:4-10*)

Behave as God's sons!

You have heard the commandment, 'You shall love your
neighbour and hate your enemy.' I say to you: love

your enemies and pray for those who persecute you; then you will be true sons of your Father in heaven; for he makes his sun rise upon bad men and good, and sends rain upon just men and unjust. If you love only those who love you, what reward is due to you? Do not even the tax-gatherers do that? And if you show friendliness only to your relatives, what more are you doing than others? Do not even the Gentiles do that? You must, therefore, be perfect as your heavenly Father is perfect.

(Mt 5:43-48)

Be patient, and hope!

I tell you truly, soon you will weep and lament, but the world will rejoice. But though you will grieve, your grief will turn to joy. When a woman is in labour, she suffers distress because her hour is come. But when she has given birth to her child, she no longer remembers her pangs, for joy that a man has been born into the world. So too with you: you are distressed at present; but I shall see you again, and your hearts will rejoice, and no one will take away your joy. *(Jn 16:20-22)*

Reflection

Obedience to rules which say 'Do not touch!' 'Do not taste!' 'Hands off!' requires self-restraint and is a form of asceticism. St Paul rejects it. But he adds that there is another kind of asceticism which Christians must practise. Because we already share in Christ's glory, *therefore,* he says, we must make our bodies dead to earthly passions.

He is telling us to become what we are — which is a paradox, yet not too obscure. What he means is this: 'You have been made and now are sons of God, cleansed of the defilement of sin, endowed with heavenly beauty and grace and glory which you cannot see; your being is good and beautiful and worthy of reverence; now live up to this dignity — be careful not to spoil God's work by unworthy conduct. You have been rescued out of the domain of darkness into Christ's kingdom of light; you must not act as if you were still sons of darkness.' Then he describes in a brief sketch the ways of darkness which Christians must avoid. All the vices that flourish in darkness and secrecy must be cast aside like an old garment, and the virtues put on instead, with charity on top like a splendid chasuble for all to see and admire.

The Christian life is a continuation of Christ's sacrifice because it requires a constant crucifixion of the flesh. Day by day, the disciple must put to death the practices of the body (cf. Rom 8:13). But this is not hard, for he has the aid of the Holy Spirit, who teaches us daily the spirit of the future kingdom and transforms us from day to day into the likeness of Christ (cf. 2 Cor 3:18).

In the passage from the Sermon on the Mount, Jesus himself describes the conduct expected of God's children. We must do better than the Jews of old, and better than the heathen around us. We must continue to love our neighbour even when he behaves like an enemy. That is the way to become a true son of God — a son who obeys his Father and becomes like him through obedience.

If we practise the kind of asceticism taught by Christ and his apostles, we can look forward to our glorification, and we *should* look forward to it, somewhat as a woman looks forward to the day when the child hidden in her womb will come forth to be seen — even as our Lady looked forward to the birth of her Son, while Christ was formed within her. This may seem a strange and daring comparison to use; but it is very much like the one which Jesus himself used at the Last Supper when looking forward to his own glorification.

Prayer

Save me, O heavenly Father, from all falseness and duplicity; in your eyes let me behave as what I am, your son; and let me truly be what in the eyes of my fellow men I seem to be, the disciple of your beloved Son Jesus Christ.

17

A Better World

St Paul's Vision

Put off your old selves and your evil ways, and put on
the new man, the nature that is being restored in the
image of its Creator and brought to know him better.
In the new humanity there is no distinction between
Greek and Jew, circumcised and uncircumcised, barbarian, Scythian, slave or free; all are in Christ and
Christ is in all. Therefore, since you are God's chosen
ones, his holy and loved ones, put on the garments of
compassion, kindness, humility, gentleness, patience; be
tolerant of one another; and be generous in forgiving, if
you have any grievances against one another. But above
all these virtues put on charity, which is the bond of
perfection; and let the peace of Christ reign in your
hearts, that peace to which you were called as members
of a single body. And be grateful.   (*Col 3:9-15*)

Christ's Command

The eleven disciples made the journey to Galilee, to the
mountain where Jesus had told them to meet him. When

they saw him they worshipped him, though some remained doubtful. Then Jesus drew near and addressed them: 'All power has been given to me in heaven and on earth,' he said. 'Go then, and convert all the nations; baptize them in the name of the Father and of the Son and of the Holy Spirit; and teach them to observe all the commandments I have given you. And be sure, I am with you always, even to the end of the world.'

(Mt 28:16-20)

Reflection

In this passage of the Epistle, St Paul is thinking not only of the transformation of the individual believer through the grace and teaching of Christ, but of a transformed humanity — a better world in which all human relationships will be penetrated by the Spirit of Christ, which is the original Wisdom of God.

For St Paul, the task of an apostle is not simply to select a few chosen souls and train them up to perfection, like rare orchids. His obligations are to all men everywhere. He looks at the whole world and sees all the great social, national and religious differences of mankind withering away as Christ's grace and his teaching prevail. He sees a new humanity arising, in which Jew and Gentile, slave and free, barbarian, Scythian, all become more and more like Christ, and therefore more and more like one another. He sees a vision of world-peace and unity, founded on love and gratitude, on forgiveness and self-control.

The alternative to self-control is passion and lust; the alternative to forgiveness is anger; the alternative to gratitude is greed and rapacity; the alternative to love is hatred; the alternative to unity is the accentuation of differences; and the alternative to peace is war, upheaval, and pathetic columns of homeless and starving refugees.

There are only two ways of life in the world, the way of light and the way of darkness. The power of Christ in the world has made it possible for men to follow the way of light effectively. St Paul looks forward to a progressive triumph of light over darkness.

If he could come back into the world today, I think he would be sorely disappointed that the grace of Christ has not made greater headway. Newman would be disappointed, too, with the English summer that has followed his second spring. But the prophetic perspective is always foreshortened. For our part, we must not underestimate the advances that have been made in the Christian era; and we must not be discouraged by the magnitude of the task still waiting to be done. The present is our opportunity. The torch of Christian life is now passed to us, and we must pass it on to others, until the whole world is lit up.

At the very end of St Matthew's gospel, Christ takes his disciples to a mountain in Galilee, 'Galilee of the Gentiles', on the fringe of the Gentile world. He stretches out his arm and says: 'Go and teach all nations....' He too had a vision of mankind renewed by baptism and by the word of his gospel. We are now his instruments for carrying on the work of justification and reconciliation. If only we could fulfil our charge as well as St Paul fulfilled his!

Prayer

We give thanks, O Lord, for all that our forefathers achieved through obedience to the gospel; may we in our turn continue the ministry of reconciliation and renewal, so that your glory may fill the whole world. Lord Jesus, Son of Man, exterminate the beasts of vice, and reign over us in peace!

18

Things Hidden from the Beginning

Transformation of the Whole

Another parable which Jesus told them was this; 'The kingdom of heaven is like leaven, which a woman takes and covers over with three measures of flour until the whole is leavened.'

All these things Jesus taught the people in parables, and he never spoke without a parable. Thus was fulfilled the word spoken by the prophet when he said: 'I shall speak in parables; I shall utter things kept secret since the foundation of the world.'   (*Mt 13:33-35*)

God's Original Intention

Some of the Pharisees came and put a question to test him: 'Can a man lawfully divorce his wife for any reason whatever?' He answered: 'Have you not read that from the beginning the Creator made them male and female and said, "For this reason a man shall leave his father and mother and shall cleave to his wife, and the two shall become one flesh"? In body they are no longer two but one. Therefore what God has joined together, let not man put asunder.'

They said to him: 'Then why did Moses lay down that a man should give a certificate of divorce when putting away his wife?' He answered: 'It was because of the hardness of your hearts that Moses allowed you to put away your wives; but originally it was not so.'

(*Mt 19:3-8*)

The Old Adam and the New

Put off your old selves and your evil ways, and put on the new man, the nature that is being restored in the image of its Creator and brought to know him better. In the new humanity there is no distinction between Greek and Jew, circumcised and uncircumcised, barbarian, Scythian, slave or free; all are in Christ and Christ is in all. Therefore, since you are God's chosen ones, his holy and loved ones, put on the garments of compassion, kindness, humility, gentleness, patience; be tolerant of one another; and be generous in forgiving, if you have any grievances against one another. But above all these virtues put on charity, which is the bond of perfection.

(*Col 3:9-14*)

Reflection

God's original intention for man was thwarted by the sin of Adam and by all the sins of his posterity. The image of God which was placed in man at his creation was marred. But through Christ, the Second Adam, who is the perfect Image of God (1:16), God's original intention is to be fulfilled. Where sin has abounded, grace will more than abound. The grace of Christ will create a new humanity in the image of the Creator.

This is not to be understood in too mystical a sense. St Paul means that the whole human scene will be transformed, and divisions will be overcome. In his enthusiasm he speaks as though it will all happen quickly, as the gospel bears its fruit throughout the world (cf. 1:6). In the parable of the leaven, Jesus speaks more prudently, but no less confidently: the leaven of the gospel will at length transform the whole mass of humanity.

One of the things kept secret since the foundation of the world, which Jesus revealed from the treasury of wisdom and knowledge hidden in his breast, was the original will of God in regard to marriage. Moses tolerated divorce, but 'from the beginning' it was not so.

From this point we can generalize. Whenever Christ 'fulfills the law' by explaining the full demands of the spirit of charity in some relationship regulated by the law, he is expressing his own original intention for mankind when he created the world and placed man in it to rule. 'You shall love your neighbour as yourself' is the original law of creation, with applications in every human relationship — between Greek and Jew, slave and free, husband and wife, parents and children. As mankind is renewed by Christ's grace, all these relationships ought to be transformed, [1] and will be transformed, until the human scene corresponds to the original intention of God the Father when he created our race through the pre-existent Christ.

Jesus himself is the prototype of the new humanity. Those who obey his teaching will become like him, com-

---

[1] This is shown in detail in *Scripture for Meditation 3: Our Divine Master*.

passionate, kind, humble, patient, ready to forgive. Without these virtues, man is not fit for the office of ruler assigned to him at the beginning (cf. Gen 1:28). He is not fit to rule over birds and beasts, let alone over his fellow men. Man is born to exercise power, but only a Christlike man can use power worthily, whether in the state, or in the Church, or in the family, or in a university or school, or in a factory, or on a farm.

Prayer

O God our Father, perfect in us the image of your Son, so that we may be gentle and patient with one another, and truly care for those over whom we have authority.

19

The Wedding Garment

Admission Free

The kingdom of heaven is like this. A king had prepared a marriage feast for his son. He sent out his servants to call those who had been invited to the wedding, but they refused to come. So he sent more servants and told them to say to the men who had been invited: 'Look! I have already prepared the banquet. My bulls and fatted calves have been slaughtered and all is ready. Pray come to the wedding.' Some ignored this message — one went off to his farm, and another to his shop; the rest seized his servants, ill-treated them, and then killed them. The king, in his anger, sent out his army and destroyed the murderers, and set fire to their city.

Then he said to his servants: 'The marriage feast is ready, but those invited were not deserving of it. Go then to the gateways of the city, and invite to the wedding everyone you find there.' So the servants went into the streets and gathered in everyone they could find, both good and bad; and the hall was filled with guests.

When the king went in to see the guests, he noticed there a man who was not wearing a wedding garment. He said to him: 'My friend, how do you come to be in here without a wedding garment?' But he remained silent. Then the king said to his servants: 'Bind him hand and foot, and throw him out into the darkness — there he can weep and gnash his teeth.' (*Mt 22:2-13*)

To those Properly Dressed

Put off your old selves and your evil ways, and put on the new man, the nature that is being restored in the image of its Creator and brought to know him better. In the new humanity there is no distinction between Greek and Jew, circumcised and uncircumcised, barbarian, Scythian, slave or free; all are in Christ and Christ is in all. Therefore, since you are God's chosen ones, his holy and loved ones, put on the garments of compassion, kindness, humility, gentleness, patience; be tolerant of one another; and be generous in forgiving, if you have any grievances against one another. But above all these virtues put on charity, which is the bond of perfection.

(*Col 3:9-14*)

Reflection

The parable contains a well known difficulty. It seems a trifle unreasonable to fetch in a man from the hedges and byways and then punish him for not being properly dressed! However, the difficulty vanishes once the allegorical sense of the parable is recognized.

The passage from Colossians provides a key to the allegory. The Gentile who has believed and has been baptized is told that he must now put off the old man with his sinful habits and put on the new habit or garb of Christ. That is to say, he must wear the garments of Christlike humility, kindness, compassion, forgiveness, and so on, with charity above all else, like a priestly chasuble. The Gentile, like the Jew, is justified by faith;

but faith alone is not sufficient clothing for those who wish to enter the kingdom. Their faith must express itself in charity and all the other Christlike virtues.

In the light of this passage, the meaning of the parable is clear enough. The Jews have rejected God's invitation; but a royal invitation is a command; therefore they will be punished for rejecting it. Their places will be taken by Gentiles called in from East and West. They are not commanded to *earn* admission, but simply to dress themselves suitably, in the virtues of Christ, which are made possible for them by the Spirit given in baptism. Whether the king in the parable offered his guests festive garments to put on, hardly matters. Certainly Christ does: the Christlike virtues are gifts of his grace.

At the ordination of a priest, when the bishop invests the candidate with the chasuble, he says: 'Take this priestly vestment, the symbol of charity.' It should be a constant reminder to the priest that his ministry is one of charity, encouragement, and reconciliation. If he preaches without love, he is like a clanging gong or a tinkling cymbal. If he lashes his hearers with verbal scorpions, he will antagonize them, destroy their good will, and drive them away. The purpose of preaching is to encourage and inspire. If a priest has no 'word of encouragement', he would do better to hold his peace. [1]

Prayer

We give you thanks, O heavenly Father, for calling us to receive an inheritance in your kingdom; clothe us, we pray, with the virtues of Christ, so that we may be found worthy of the honour which you have promised to us.

---

[1] Cf. Acts 13 : 13-16, quoted above, p. 10.

20

The Word
in the Community

The Word has many Forms

Be grateful. Let Christ's word which dwells within you
display its wealth: teach and admonish one another with
all wisdom; show to God the gratitude of your hearts by
singing psalms, hymns and spiritual canticles. Whatever
you do and whatever you say, do all in the name of the
Lord Jesus, and give thanks to God the Father through
him.   *(Col 3:15-17)*

The Harvest of the Word

A sower went out to sow, and as he sowed, some of the
seed fell by the wayside, and birds came and ate it. Some
fell on rocky ground where there was little earth, and it
sprouted at once because it had not sunk deep in the
soil; but when the sun rose, it was dried up and withered,
because it had no roots. Some fell among briars, and the
briars grew up and choked it, and it yielded nothing.

But some fell into good soil; this came up and grew and yielded a crop, producing up to thirty, sixty, and a hundred-fold. (*Mk 4:3-8*)

A Word for Bearers of the Word

You are the salt of the earth. (But if salt loses its taste, what will you use to restore its saltiness? It is no longer good for anything except to be thrown out and trampled under men's feet.) You are the light of the world. A city built on a mountain-top cannot but be seen. When a lamp is lit, it is not put under a barrel, but on a lamp-stand; then it gives light to everyone in the house. You too, in the same way, must let your light shine out before men, so that they will see your good works and give glory to your Father in heaven. (*Mt 5:13-16*)

Reflection

The 'word of Christ' is the teaching of Christ or the Wisdom of Christ. This Word or Wisdom created order at the beginning, when God reduced chaos to cosmos by his Word. The same Word is to be released in each Christian community to do its creative work of producing light, order and life.

Christ is a prophet (and much more than a prophet), raised up among mankind to teach the many what they do not know by nature or instinct, namely, how to live together in peace, friendliness and happiness. His Wisdom is 'the light of the world' and 'the salt of the earth'. But these titles can also be transferred to the disciples as bearers of the word, so long as they maintain it in its purity and make it heard. They are the light of the world because they show the many how to live in the various relationships in which their lives are set; and they are the salt of the earth because their teaching will preserve these relationships from decay and give them savour.

But the word of Christ, to have its effect, must be constantly uttered and constantly heard. The gift of the Spirit resembles alcohol in that it loosens men's tongues (cf. Acts 2:13) and makes them speak to one another. In a Christian community there must be an abundance of words. Government is not by coercion; those who rule and lead others must rely on the power which truth has over men of good will (cf. Jn 18:37). Therefore they must speak out in words of encouragement, gratitude, instruction and correction.

When St Paul says that 'the word of Christ must dwell in you richly', he may mean 'in such a way as to produce an abundant harvest — thirty, sixty or a hundred-fold', or he may mean 'in a rich variety of forms'. As the Author of the Epistle to the Hebrews says, in the Old Testament God revealed himself 'in many portions and in many ways'. This phrase can be transferred to Christian preaching. We can never express the whole mystery of Christ in one literary form, or the whole of his teaching in one book. His word must constantly find partial expression in a variety of forms.

St Paul mentions both first and last 'thanksgiving', by which he means in the first place eucharistic prayers addressed to God. We have abundant reasons for gratitude to God who created and restored us through Christ. We are made in his image, capable of addressing him in words, and invited to address him in words. His invitation should be regarded as a royal command and joyfully obeyed. It is a privilege to enter into communion with him through words of thanks and praise.

But we are also indebted to one another. The foot cannot live without the hand, or the hand without the belly, and so on. We should be grateful to one another. But gratitude which does not express itself is worthless.

It *must* find expression in words, or it wilts and ceases to exist. To words of gratitude must be added words of instruction and where necessary words of admonition. According to St Paul, in our prayers to God, words of petition should always be combined with words of gratitude. In the same way, it is wisdom to combine words of admonition with words of gratitude and praise when we speak to one another.

Again like alcohol, the Spirit of Christ will move Christians to *sing*. Unfortunately, there is an ambiguity in the Greek here. Word for word, St Paul seems to say: 'You are to sing in your hearts to God'. But he does not mean that our singing is to be entirely interior, and audible to God alone. When he was imprisoned with Silas at Philippi, the two of them sang psalms in the night which were heard by the other prisoners (cf. Acts 16: 25). What he means is *'from* your hearts' or *'with* your hearts'. The hymn-singing of a Christian community should not be a mournful formality. It should be full-throated song, coming from the diaphragm, manifesting the singer's desire to fulfil in this way his duty to praise God.

No doubt the first generation in its enthusiasm produced an abundance of psalms, hymns and spiritual canticles. It is sad that only fragments have survived. But every generation must make its own hymns, and sing them with a will. Singing is one of the best ways of keeping Christ's word audible in the community.

Prayer

Inspire us, O heavenly Father, to pray to you as we should, and to be duly grateful to you and to one another. Give us leaders endowed with wisdom and speech, so that we may live in order and peace, according to your will.

21

The Christian Household

Sanctifying the Home

Wives: be subject to your husbands, as is right in the Lord. Husbands: love your wives, and do not be bitter to them. Children: obey your parents in everything — that is the way to please the Lord. Fathers: do not vex your children, or their spirit may be broken. Slaves: obey your human masters in everything, and work not only when watched or for the sake of human praise, but with simple honesty, in fear of the Lord. Whatever you do, do it with a will, remembering that you are doing it for the Lord rather than for men; and be sure that the Lord will give you an inheritance as your reward. The Lord whose slaves you are is Christ. No matter who does wrong, he will pay the penalty for his misdeed; with God there is no favouritism. Masters: treat your slaves justly and fairly, bearing in mind that you too have a Master in heaven.   (*Col 3:18—4:1*)

Christ's Words for Husbands

You have heard the commandment, 'You shall not commit adultery.' I tell you that anyone who looks at a woman with desire has already committed adultery with her, in his heart.

If your right eye causes you to sin, pluck it out, throw it away! Better for you that one part of your body should perish than the whole of it be thrown into hell. If your right hand causes you to sin, chop it off, throw it away! Better for you that one part of your body should perish than that the whole of it should go into hell.

It was laid down that 'whoever puts away his wife must give her a certificate of divorce.' But I tell you that to put away your wife (unless the union was illicit[1]) is to make an adultress of her, and to marry a woman who has been put away is to commit adultery.   (*Mt 5:27-32*)

Reflection

This section of the Epistle is disappointingly brief and sketchy. After all that St Paul has said about the treasures of wisdom made available to us in Christ, we might hope that he would take time to describe in greater detail the wonderful transformation of domestic, civil and political life which can be expected where Christ's words are heard and obeyed. Instead, he gives us a brief sketch of the Christian household with particular emphasis on the obedience of slaves. There is nothing radical or revolutionary about it. The Christian household will conform to contemporary patterns. Wives, children and slaves will obey the master of the house, as in any Stoic

---

[1] On the meaning of this exceptive clause, see *The Way* 8 (1968), pp. 314-315.

G

household. All that is different is that in addition to motives of natural morality, the Christian wife, child or slave will obey 'in the Lord', that is, to please the Lord, and in a spirit of Christian love.

The conservatism of St Paul is plain, particularly in the words which he addressed to slaves. He does not call in question the whole institution of slavery, whereby one man owns another and can buy and sell him like an ox or an ass. On this point, the Holy Spirit seems to have left Paul's conscience undisturbed. What he says to slaves is designed to help them to acquiesce in the status quo and turn it to their spiritual profit. He promises them an inheritance in the world to come, but holds out no hope that their Christian masters will feel obliged to give them a stake in this world too. His advice to slave-owners is that they should grant justice and equality to their slaves. He does not mean 'equality with their master' or they would cease to be slaves. He means that a master must treat all his slaves alike, without favouritism. His aim is the amelioration and sanctification of the status quo by the introduction of supernatural motives to support what is already socially acceptable. It can hardly be said that Paul speaks with the courage of a prophet on this point.

How much more challenging are the words which Jesus himself addresses to husbands in the Sermon on the Mount! Here is frank recognition that the break-up of families often comes from the lust and hard-heartedness of the master of the house, who rules his wife by the threat of divorce and seeks his pleasure elsewhere. For such men Christ has stern words — as stern as any he spoke. By contrast, all that St Paul has to say to husbands is: 'Love your wives, and do not be bitter to them.' After all that he has said about the renewal of mankind through the coming of God's Son, this seems inadequate. The renewal of the world must begin in the family, and the renewal of the family must begin with the establishment of a right relationship between husband and wife. It seems hardly sufficient just to say that wives must be obedient and husbands must not be bitter.

If St Paul is the author of the Epistle to the Ephesians, he must have recognized the inadequacy of his treatment of family relationships in Colossians. Ephesians is largely a paraphrase of Colossians, until it reaches this point of family relationships, where a much more positive doctrine of married love is proposed. If, on the other hand, the Epistle to the Ephesians is the work of a disciple of Paul's, as many commentators think, this disciple must have recognized that the few maxims given in Colossians are hardly commensurate with the importance of the subject.

Prayer

Stir up our consciences, O Lord, so that we will not acquiesce in situations which ought to be changed. Grant that we may appreciate and be grateful for what is good in our inheritance; but give us, too, the courage to condemn and demolish what needs to be rebuilt.

22

Watching and Praying

Perseverance in Prayer

Persevere in prayer, and in your vigils offer thanks. Pray too for me, that God may open the door for me to preach and to proclaim as I should the mystery of Christ — for which I am now in prison. *(Col 4:2-4)*

Praying at Night

Then he came to the disciples and found them sleeping. He said to Peter: 'Could you not keep watch one hour with me? Watch and pray, that you may not yield to temptation. The spirit indeed is willing, but the flesh is weak.' Again he left them and prayed a second time: 'My Father, if this chalice cannot pass away but I must drink it, may thy will be done.' Then he came again and found the disciples sleeping, for their eyes were heavy. *(Mt 26:40-43)*

Who opens the door?

Be on your guard, then, watch and pray; for you do not know when is the appointed time. It is as when a man leaves his home and goes abroad: he gives authority to his servants, assigns to each his special task, and tells the doorkeeper to keep watch. Watch, therefore, for you do not know when the master of the house is coming. It may be evening or midnight or cock-crow or morning. Watch then, or he may come suddenly and find you asleep. *(Mk 13:33-37)*

See, I stand knocking at the door. If anyone hears my voice and opens the door, I will come inside and share a meal with him, and he with me. *(Apoc 3:20)*

Reflection

St Paul's exhortation to watch and pray bears a certain resemblance to Jesus' words to his disciples in Gethsemane — which suggests that Jesus' words were understood to have reference not only to the special situation in Gethsemane, but to Christian prayer in general. Perhaps he wished his disciples to make a habit of watching at night, for long periods — say, an hour or two — to pray that God's will may be done and that they may not succumb to temptation.

There are also certain parables in which Jesus exhorts his disciples to 'watch'. These are usually taken as exhortations to be ready for judgment — to be leading a well-ordered life in obedience to Christ's teaching and in fulfilment of one's office. However, the same imagery could be applied to prayer: we must watch in prayer for long periods, so as to be ready at the moment when the Lord knocks, to open the door and invite him in to sup with us.

On another occasion, Jesus pictures the person praying as being outside the door knocking (cf. Mt 7:7). He must persevere for a long time, so as to be still there at the moment when the door is opened. It seems that the idea of the *kairos* or 'right time' has its application not only to belief in the gospel, but also to prayer. A man does not have the gospel preached to him every day; he has his *kairos* and must seize it before it passes, or it will be too late. Christ's parables, and his words in Gethsemane suggest that we must spend lengthy periods watching at night so that when the divine afflatus comes we may be ready to catch it and cooperate with the Holy Spirit. We must wait patiently, like the sick at Bethesda (cf. Jn 5:4), for the coming of the Spirit to stir up the springs of our consciousness and enable us to pray as we ought.

In this passage of the Epistle, St Paul makes another application of the image of the closed door. He invites the Colossians to join with him in praying that God will open the gate of his prison, and open the gate of speech, and open up a field of apostolic activity, so that he can reveal the secret wisdom of Christ as he ought.

The word 'persevere' implies that prayer requires patience and long effort, and is constantly beset by the temptation to give up. We must wait and wait, humbly repeating some simple words, as Christ did in Gethsemane, until God in his own good time will send an angel or one of the unpredictable gusts of his Spirit to raise us up to pray 'as we ought' (Rom. 8:26).

Prayer

Give us the patience, O heavenly Father, to persevere in prayer, so that we may be ready for the moments when your Holy Spirit will lift the wings of our souls and enable us to pray as we ought. Come to us often, or our courage will flag, and we shall succumb to the temptation of sleep.

23

The Church
and the World

Paul's Advice

Show wisdom in your relations with those outside, and
so redeem the time. What you say to them must be seasoned with the salt of courtesy; and you must know
how each questioner is to be answered.   (*Col 4:5-6*)

The Words of Christ

You are the light of the world. A city built on a
mountain-top cannot but be seen. When a lamp is lit, it
is not put under a barrel, but on a lampstand; then it
gives light to everyone in the house. You too, in the
same way, must let your light shine out before men, so
that they will see your good works and give glory to your
Father in heaven.   (*Mt 5:14-16*)

The Prayer of Christ

Not for these alone do I pray, but for those too who through their word will believe in me: may they all be one; may they too be in us, as you, Father, in me and I in you, that the world may believe that it was you who sent me. The glory which you gave me, I have given to them, that they may be one, as we are one. I in them, and you in me, that they may be perfectly one, that the world may know that it was you who sent me, and that you have loved them as you loved me. *(Jn 17:20-23)*

The First Disciples

All who had become believers gathered in one place and shared everything in common. They sold their property and estates and divided the money among all, according to each one's needs. Day by day they continued to worship together in the temple; and they broke bread at home, and shared their meals with joy and simplicity of heart; thus they gave praise to God and enjoyed the goodwill of all the people. And day by day the Lord added to the community those who were to be saved.

(Acts 2:44-47)

Reflection

Here again the brief words of St Paul are far less challenging than those of Christ. He seems to assume that the Colossian Christians will be known as such by their pagan neighbours, and that their neighbours will question them about their beliefs and practices. They must be ready to give a courteous answer, 'seasoned with salt'. If salt is here a metaphor for wit, presumably the sense is that their replies must be brief and interesting, for brevity is the soul of wit. They must not be long and boring, but vivid and memorable, like the words of Christ. They must also be appropriate to the questioner. As Christ said, pearls must not be cast before swine. By observing these few rules the Colossian disciples will behave with 'wisdom' towards those outside, and in this way they will 'redeem the time'.

'Redeeming the time' is a fine, salty phrase. Its meaning and relevance are not too obvious, but at least it is not dull. If the Epistle to the Ephesians is the work of a disciple, he probably took this phrase to mean 'redeeming your contemporaries', because he adds 'for the days are evil' (hence in need of redemption). If the Christian speaks courteously and prudently in defending his faith, he will rescue his pagan neighbours from the darkness of idolatry. However, the phrase may simply mean 'making full use of your opportunities'.

St Paul does not here suggest that the *conduct* of Gentile Christians should be a light shining out before all men. He does not tell them to become social pioneers like the early disciples at Jerusalem, who tried to fulfil the prayer of Christ by breaking down the barriers between rich and poor. Those early experiments had failed, and could not be held up as an example to the Gentiles. But it is difficult to avoid the feeling that St Paul has tamed the gospel and domesticated it. The local church is becoming highly respectable, and perhaps a little too worried about its image. The Christian must be careful not to upset anyone or put anyone off. He must be nice to unbelievers, and pleasant in conversation.

It is a pity that St Paul said so little about the social obligations of Christianity. Christians have always turned to his Epistles for guidance and have found in them little or no encouragement to attempt the reform of social customs and institutions outside the home. It is refreshing to turn back to the words of Christ and of John the Baptist, whose social conscience was much more sensitive.

Prayer

Lord Jesus, source of wisdom, inspire the present leaders
of your Church to fill up what is wanting in the social
teaching of our tradition, so that our light may shine
out before men and help to redeem our time.

24

Paul and his Assistants

Words of Commendation

All the news of me will be given you by Tychicus, our
beloved brother and faithful helper and fellow-servant
in the Lord. I have sent him to you specially so that you
will have news of me, and he will encourage your hearts.
With him I am sending Onesimus, our faithful and beloved brother, who is one of your number. These two
will tell you all about the situation here. My fellow-
prisoner Aristarchus sends greetings. So does Mark, the
cousin of Barnabas; you have received instructions about
him: if he visits you, make him welcome. Jesus Justus
too sends greetings. These are my only helpers in the
work of God's kingdom; they have been a comfort to
me. Greetings too from your own Epaphras, a servant
of Christ Jesus, who is ever striving in prayer for you
that you may stand firm in perfect fulfilment of all God's
will. I assure you that he toils mightily for you and for
the brethren in Laodicea, and those in Hierapolis. Our
dear Luke, the doctor, greets you, as also does Demas.

(Col 4:7-14)

Paul, Mark and Barnabas

After a certain time, Paul said to Barnabas: 'Let us go back and visit the brethren in all the cities in which we preached the word of the Lord, to see how they are.' Barnabas wanted to bring John Mark too, but Paul did not think it right that they should take with them one who had deserted them in Pamphilia and had not gone with them to their task. [1] There was a sharp quarrel, and the result was that they separated from each other. Barnabas took Mark with him and sailed to Cyprus. Paul chose Silas and set out on his journey, after the brethren had commended him to the grace of the Lord.
(Acts 15:36-40)

The Clash at Antioch

But when Cephas came to Antioch, I resisted him face to face, because he was self-condemned. For before the arrival of certain persons from James, he had been taking his meals with the Gentiles; but after their arrival, he began to draw back and set himself apart, fearing those of the circumcision. The other Jews played the hypocrite along with him — so much so that even Barnabas was swept along with them by their hypocrisy. But when I saw that they were not walking steadily according to the truth of the gospel, I said to Cephas in the presence of them all: 'If you, who were born a Jew, live as a Gentile and not as a Jew, how can you compel the Gentiles to judaize?'
(Gal 2:11-14)

Reflection

This passage of the Epistle presents two problems, which may be connected with each other: Why was Epaphras

---

[1] Cf. Acts 13:14, quoted above, p. 10.

so worried about the constancy of the newly founded church? And why does St Paul have to lament that he has so few Jewish assistants?

The answer may be that these are results of Paul's intervention at Antioch, when he attacked Peter in public and accused him of 'compelling the Gentiles to judaize'. This incident probably took place about 54 A.D., just before Paul set out on his third journey. [1] If so, it was quite recent history at the time when he wrote to the Colossians.

Paul's behaviour on that occasion must have shocked the Jewish Christians who held Peter in veneration. It continues to shock some commentators to this day. At Antioch, 'even Barnabas', one of the pioneers of the Gentile missions, sided with Peter. It is probable that Paul found himself isolated and even cold-shouldered by the Jewish brethren. He never returned to Antioch after 54, and when he arrived in Jerusalem, he was warned by James the brother of the Lord that the many thousands of Jewish believers present in the city were incensed against him (cf. Acts 21:20-21).

Epaphras may have heard from Mark what happened at Antioch, and from others how sorely the Galatian churches had been upset by anti-pauline accounts of the incident. If so, the cause of Epaphras's anxiety will be that he fears his work at Colossae may be undone when the brethren at Colossae hear of Paul's protest at Antioch. If this is the situation, it is plain why St Paul wrote this exposition of his gospel of Gentile freedom: he is trying to forestall a Galatian-type crisis in the Phrygian churches.

Tychicus is commended to the Colossians as 'a beloved brother and fellow-servant in Christ', Onesimus as 'a faithful and beloved brother', and Aristarchus as

---

[1] Cf. *Galatians,* pp. 16 and 178.

'my fellow-captive'. For Mark there is no special formula of commendation, simply a statement that if he comes to Colossae, he is to be made welcome. Apparently he is no longer in disgrace, and he is reckoned among the Jewish helpers who have been a comfort to Paul; but one misses a kindly word such as 'our beloved son' or 'brother'. [1] Presumably Barnabas had sent Mark to look after Paul in his imprisonment. Everything that we know about Barnabas is to his credit.

Prayer

Heavenly Father, unite in firm bonds of love all who share the task of spreading the gospel. Free us from jealousies and rivalries, and make us prompt to forgive one another's failings.

---

[1] In 2 Tim 4:11 he is described rather coldly as 'a useful assistant to me'.

25

Linking the Churches

The House-Church at Laodicea

Greetings to the brethren at Laodicea, and to Nympha and the church that meets at her house. After this letter has been read out to you, have it read also in the church of Laodicea, and obtain the letter which I have sent to Laodicea and have that read out to you. Say to Archippus: 'Remember the ministry you have received in the Lord, and be sure to fulfil it.' I, Paul, greet you with my own hand. Remember that I am in prison. Grace be with you!
(Col 4:15-18)

Seek a Worthy Household

When you go into a city or village, inquire after a worthy household, and lodge there until you leave. Bless the house when you go in; if the household is worthy, let your peace be upon it; but if not, let it return to you. If any house or town will not receive you, and will not listen to your words, as you go out of that house or city, shake the dust off your feet. I tell you truly, the day of judgment will be more bearable for the land of Sodom and Gomorrha than for that city! *(Mt 10:11-15)*

The House-Church at Corinth

Brethren, you are aware that the members of the household of Stephanas were the first fruits of the harvest in Greece, and have devoted themselves to the service of God's people. I beg you, therefore, to show deference to such persons, and indeed to all who share in our toils and labours.   (*1 Cor 16:15-16*)

Reflection

When Paul or Epaphras or any other missionary founded a church in a Greek city, the little community would meet at the house of one of the more affluent brethren. When Jesus told his disciples to choose a 'worthy' house, he meant in the first place a house of good repute, but also a spacious house where the Eucharist could be celebrated becomingly — just as he himself commandeered 'a large upper room well furnished' for the Last Supper (cf. Mk 14:15). At Corinth, the house of Stephanas became the 'church' (cf. 1 Cor 11:22); at Philippi, the house of Lydia (cf. Acts 16:40); at Ephesus, the house of Aquila and Priscilla (cf. 1 Cor 16:19); at Laodicea, the house of Nympha and Archippus (Col 4:15-16); and at Colossae, the house of Philemon.

It was natural that the owners of these households should become leaders of the congregations. Formal appointment was hardly necessary. At the end of First Corinthians (16:15), we learn that the household of Stephanas at Corinth 'appointed themselves to the ministry'. St Paul approves, since he calls upon the rest to obey them. At Laodicea (or perhaps at Colossae) Archippus has received the ministry. St Paul has a special word for him: 'Remember the ministry you have received in the Lord and be sure to fulfil it.' But he does not say this directly to Archippus. He tells the other members of the church to say it to him — doubtless in order to ensure willing obedience on the part of these others, and to make Archippus's task as leader of the church so much the easier for him. It appears that the ministry was appointed very informally in these tiny churches. One or two families would become the 'pillars of the parish' and these would of necessity supply the leadership and preside at meetings of the church.

In arranging for the exchange of letters between Colossae and Laodicea, St Paul probably wished to ensure contact or continued contact between the leaders of the two churches — for their mutual encouragement and for the preservation of the true gospel, as taught by Paul and Epaphras.

Prayer

May your peace descend and remain, O Lord, upon every household that proves itself a pillar of its parish; raise up from such families men to offer themselves for the ministry of your people, and grant them the wisdom which leadership requires.

26

Social and Religious Freedom

The Epistle to Philemon

From Paul, a prisoner, for Christ Jesus, and the brother Timothy, to our good friend and helper Philemon, to our sister Apphia, to our comrade Archippus, and to the church that meets at your house: grace and peace be upon you all from God our Father and from the Lord Jesus Christ.

I thank my God and constantly remember you in my prayers, because I hear of your love and faith towards the Lord Jesus and towards all God's people. I pray that the faith in which you share may enable you to recognize all the good which is in your power to accomplish for Christ's sake. Your charity has been a source of great joy and consolation to me, brother, because I have heard how you have gladdened the hearts of God's people.

Therefore, although I have in Christ full liberty to lay down for you what is your duty, yet I prefer to appeal to your charity as Paul an old man, now also a prisoner for Christ Jesus. I appeal to you on behalf of this child of mine, begotten in imprisonment — I mean Onesimus. He was once useless to you, but is now useful [1] both to you and to me. I am sending him back to you; pray make him welcome. He has become a part of me.

I should have liked to keep him with me, to serve me in place of you, while I am imprisoned for the gospel. However, I decided not to do anything without your consent. I prefer that the good which you do should be done freely and not under constraint. Perhaps the reason why he was parted from you for a while was that you should have him back again for ever, no longer as a slave but as more than a slave, a beloved brother.

He is very dear to me; how much more dear should he be to you, to whom he belongs by ordinary ownership and in the Lord as well? If then you regard my wishes as yours, welcome him as you would myself. If he has done you any wrong or owes you anything, transfer the debt to me. I sign with my own hand: I will repay it, PAUL. (I will not mention that you owe me your very self!) Yes, brother, let me have this kindness from you in the Lord. Gladden my heart in Christ! I have written to you with full confidence in your readiness to comply, and am sure that you will do even more than I ask.

One other request: that you will prepare somewhere for me to stay, for I hope that through your prayers I shall be spared for you. Greetings to you from Epaphras, my fellow-prisoner for Christ Jesus, and from my helpers, Mark, Aristarchus, Demas and Luke. The grace of our Lord Jesus Christ be with your spirit. Amen.

---

[1] St Paul is here punning on the name 'Onesimus', which means 'Helpful'.

Advice for Christian Slaves

Let each one remain in the condition in which he was when called. If you were a slave when called, do not let that trouble you (but if you have the opportunity to become free, it is better to use it*). For a man who was a slave when called by the Lord becomes the Lord's freedman; and one who was free when called becomes Christ's slave. You have been bought at great cost; do not become slaves to any human master. Let each one of you remain, brethren, in the same condition in which he was when called.   (*1 Cor 7:20-24*)

* *The Greek here is ambiguous. It can also mean the exact opposite: 'If you have an opportunity to become free, choose rather to stay as you are.' St Paul is obscure because embarrassed. He cannot recommend a slave to seek manumission without being inconsistent with his principle laid down in v. 20.*

Reflection

Philemon appears to be a member of the community of Colossae (cf. Col 4:9). There is no reason to think that St Paul has ever met him (cf. Col 2:2). One of his slaves, Onesimus by name, has run away. St Paul has converted him to Christianity, and is sending him back to his master, in company with Tychicus, the bearer of the Epistle to the Colossians. [1] The rest of the story has to be filled in by conjecture.

It seems that when Onesimus made his bid for freedom, he stole money or valuables from Philemon's house,

---

[1] Compare Col 4:7-14 with Philemon 23-24. Paul has the same companions with him in both cases.

and when he had used up his stolen substance, he began to wish he were back home again. Being afraid to go back, he sought out Paul and asked his intercession. (He must have heard of Paul while still in the house of Philemon, but he was not then converted.) Paul, being in prison, kept him for a time and made use of his services, and in the meanwhile instructed and baptized him.

He is now sending him back to his master with Tychicus and with this letter of commendation and intercession. Paul pleads for him as for his own son, asks Philemon to receive him as a brother, and accepts as his own whatever debt Onesimus has incurred by his theft. He does not expect to have to pay the debt, but by his offer he enables Philemon to make a gift to himself by remitting the debt. He also hints that he would be glad if Philemon would manumit Onesimus and send him back; Paul would be glad to have his services again.

The letter is often praised as a model of Christian tact — though perhaps it might have been still more tactful if the second half of v. 19 had been omitted ('I will not mention that you owe me your very self'). But it probably owes its inclusion in the canon of Scripture to the light which it casts on St Paul's attitude to slavery. He does not condemn the institution of slavery root and branch, but urges that the relationship between the Christian master and his Christian slave be governed by brotherly charity. Philemon is asked to look upon his runaway slave as a beloved brother. St Paul does not, however, draw what to us would seem the obvious conclusion — that if one's brother is a slave, one must make every effort to liberate him.

In the passage from First Corinthians, St Paul permits a Christian slave to accept manumission if it is offered. But the explanation which follows does not explain this permission. It explains why one who is called as a slave should not worry about his servile condition and should not feel that he is a second-class member of the Church: the Christian slave is the Lord's freedman, and the Christian free man is the Lord's slave. The implication is that in the Lord's eyes the Christian slave and the Christian free man have the same standing; they must remember their real equality before God. These considerations will help both master and slave to feel comfortable within the status quo.

St Paul's reason for urging acceptance of the status quo was that he believed the end of the world to be imminent: 'the time is short....the fabric of this world is passing away' (1 Cor 7: 29,31). Whereas for Christ and for John the Baptist eschatology provided a motive for change ('Repent, for the kingdom of heaven is at hand'), for St Paul it has become a reason for tolerating the status quo. Now that we no longer expect the Return of Christ and the End of the Age in the near future, we can no longer be content with the apostle's social conservatism. We must listen to the social teaching of the Popes, and do all in our power to create social institutions, structures and services which embody the precept of brotherly love as explained by Christ our Master.

Prayer

May your Holy Spirit quicken the consciences of all good men throughout the world, O Lord of all, so that we may level out the inequalities of wealth and share as brothers in the fruits of the earth which you have placed at our disposal.

Appendix

THE EPISTLE TO THE COLOSSIANS

1 From Paul, by the will of God an apostle of Jesus Christ, and the brother Timothy, ² to God's people at Colossae, our brethren through faith in Christ: grace and peace be upon you from God our Father.

³ We give thanks to God, the Father of our Lord Jesus Christ, every time we think of you in our prayers, ⁴ for we have heard of your faith in Christ Jesus and of the charity which you bear to all God's people, ⁵ a charity that springs from your hope for the blessings stored up for you in heaven, as you have heard in the message of truth ⁶ which the gospel brought among you. It is the same everywhere: the gospel bears fruit and thrives the world over, as it has done among you, ever since the day when you first heard it and recognized it as being truly a grace offered you by God. ⁷ You were taught it by my beloved fellow-servant Epaphras, who has been a faithful servant of Christ on my behalf. ⁸ It is he who has told me of the charity inspired in you by the Holy Spirit.

⁹ From the day when I first heard of you, I have never ceased to pray for you. I pray that you may receive that fulness of spiritual understanding which brings perfect knowledge of God's will, ¹⁰ so that your manner of life may be worthy of the Lord and pleasing to him in every way. ¹¹ I pray that you may bear fruit in every good work as you advance in the knowledge of God. I pray that through his glorious power God will fill you with all strength to face the future with endurance, with fortitude, ¹² and with joyful gratitude to the Father who

has made us fit to share the inheritance of his people in the kingdom of light. [13] For he has rescued us from the domain of darkness, and set us in the kingdom of his beloved Son, [14] in whom we have received redemption, the forgiveness of our sins.

[15] He is the visible Image of the invisible God, born before all creation; [16] for through him everything in heaven and on earth, things visible and invisible, thrones, lordships, powers and authorities — all were created through him and for him. [17] Before all things were, he is; and all things are held in being by him. [18] He is, too, the head of the body which is the Church — he who is its beginning, the first of the dead to be reborn. Thus in everything his rank is preeminent. [19] It pleased God to place all perfection in him, [20] and through him to reconcile the universe to himself, all that is on earth and all that is in heaven, when he made peace through his blood, shed on the cross. [21] Your own hearts were once hostile and estranged from God through your misdeeds; [22] but now God has reconciled you to himself through Christ's death in his body of flesh, in order to make you holy in his sight, free from blemish and free from guilt.

[23] Only you must remain firm and steadfast in your faith, immovably attached to the hope held out to you by the gospel which you have heard — the gospel that has been proclaimed to the whole creation under heaven, the gospel of which I, Paul, am a minister. [24] At present I am suffering for your sake, and I am glad of it. I am helping to pay off in my person, on behalf of his body which is the Church, that which is wanting to Christ's afflictions. [25] I have been appointed minister of this Church, in virtue of the office assigned me by God for your benefit, to make fully known the word of God, [26] the mystery that was hidden through the ages and the generations, but is now revealed to God's people. [27] To them God has been pleased to make known the generosity of his glorious design among the Gentiles, namely, that Christ is in your midst and is your hope of glory. [28] He is the one whom we preach. We admonish all mankind, and instruct all mankind in all wisdom, so as to lead all mankind to maturity in Christ. [29] That is the end for which I labour and strive, through the strength of him who works in me with power.

2 [1] I want you to know how great a contest I am undergoing — for your sake, for those at Laodicea, and for all others who have not seen me in person, [2] that their hearts may take courage, that they may be united in charity and enriched with perfect understanding, and so attain to full knowledge of God's mystery — that is, to full knowledge of Christ, [3] in whom all the treasures of wisdom and knowledge are concealed. [4] I say this so that no one will mislead you with persuasive talk. [5] Although I am absent in body, I am with you in spirit, and I rejoice to see your good order and the firmness of your faith in Christ.

[6] Since the message delivered to you was that Christ Jesus is Lord, live your lives in union with him, [7] rooted in him, founded on him. Hold fast to the faith in the form in which you were taught it, and be abundantly grateful for it. [8] Watch that no one captivates you with philosophy and empty deceit — with man-made wisdom which would subject you to the elemental powers of the world and not to Christ. [9] For the fulness of the Godhead dwells in his body, [10] and in union with him you lack nothing. He is the head of every power and principality.

[11] In him you have received a spiritual circumcision, not a surgical operation for the removal of bodily flesh, but Christ's circumcision. [12] You have been buried with him through your faith in the power of God who raised him from the dead. [13] You too were once dead, because of your sins and because your natural being was uncircumcised; but God has restored you to life with Christ, by forgiving all your sins, [14] by cancelling the invoice of debts to the law which stood against us, nailing it to the cross. [15] He has disarmed the powers and dominations and made a public spectacle of them, leading them as prisoners in his triumph.

[16] Therefore let no one call you to account for what you eat or drink, or for the observance of festivals, new moons or sabbaths. [17] These things were but the shadow of what was to come; the reality is Christ. [18] If anyone claims to have had visions, and then with affected self-abasement advocates the worship of angels, he must not be allowed to impose his will on you. Such a teacher is puffed out with the futile conceits of his own natural mind; [19] he has not maintained union with the head from which the whole body, through its joints and ligaments, is supplied with nourishment, given solidity and made to fill out as God would have it grow. [20] If you have died with Christ and escaped from subjection to the elements of the world, why live as if you still belonged to the world? Why let men make rules for you: [21] 'Do not touch this! Do

not taste that! Do not handle the other!' — 22 rules concerning only material things which perish in the very use? Would you follow human doctrines and precepts? 23 They have an appearance of wisdom, with their talk of 'voluntary veneration', 'self-abasement', and 'corporal austerity'; but they are of no true worth, and lead only to gratification of the natural man.

3 1 If you have risen with Christ, seek the things that are above, where Christ is seated at God's right hand. 2 Set your thoughts on heavenly things, not on the things of earth. 3 For you are dead! And your life is hidden with Christ in God.

4 The day will come when Christ, who is our life, will be revealed; then you too will be revealed with him in glory. 5 Therefore make your bodies dead to earthly passions: have done with fornication, impurity, lust, evil desires, and that greed for money which is a form of idolatry. 6 Those are the things which bring down God's anger. 7 You yourselves once walked that way, when you lived that kind of life. 8 But now you must strip yourselves of every vice, of anger, passion and baseness; cleanse your lips of profane and vulgar speech; 9 and do not tell lies to one another. Put off your old selves and your evil ways, 10 and put on the new man, the nature that is being restored in the image of its Creator and brought to know him better.

11 In the new humanity there is no distinction between Greek and Jew, circumcised and uncircumcised, barbarian, Scythian, slave or free; all are in Christ and Christ is in all. 12 Therefore, since you are God's chosen ones, his holy and loved ones, put on the garments of compassion, kindness, humility, gentleness, patience; 13 be tolerant of one another; and be generous in forgiving, if you have any grievances against one another. 14 But above all these virtues put on charity, which is the bond of perfection; 15 and let the peace of Christ reign in your hearts, that peace to which you were called as members of a single body. And be grateful.

16 Let Christ's word which dwells within you display its wealth: teach and admonish one another with all wisdom; show to God the gratitude of your hearts by singing psalms, hymns and spiritual canticles. 17 Whatever you do and whatever you say, do all in the name of the Lord Jesus, and give thanks to God the Father through him.

¹⁸ Wives: be subject to your husbands, as is right in the Lord. ¹⁹ Husbands: love your wives, and do not be bitter to them. ²⁰ Children: obey your parents in everything — that is the way to please the Lord. ²¹ Fathers: do not vex your children, or their spirit may be broken. ²² Slaves: obey your human masters in everything, and work not only when watched or for the sake of human praise, but with simple honesty, in fear of the Lord. ²³ Whatever you do, do it with a will, remembering that you are doing it for the Lord rather than for men; ²⁴ and be sure that the Lord will give you an inheritance as your reward. The Lord whose slaves you are is Christ. ²⁵ No matter who does wrong, he will pay the penalty for his misdeed; with God there is no favouritism. 4 ¹ Masters: treat your slaves justly and fairly, bearing in mind that you too have a Master in heaven.

²Persevere in prayer, and in your vigils offer thanks. ³ Pray too for me, that God may open the door for me ⁴ to preach and to proclaim as I should the mystery of Christ — for which I am now in prison. ⁵ Show wisdom in your relations with those outside, and so redeem the time. ⁶ What you say to them must be seasoned with the salt of courtesy; and you must know how each questioner is to be answered.

⁷ All the news of me will be given you by Tychicus, our beloved brother and faithful helper and fellow-servant in the Lord. ⁸ I have sent him to you specially so that you will have news of me, and he will encourage your hearts. ⁹ With him I am sending Onesimus, our faithful and beloved brother, who is one of your number. These two will tell you all about the situation here. ¹⁰ My fellow-prisoner Aristarchus sends his greetings. So does Mark, the cousin of Barnabas; you have received instructions about him: if he visits you, make him welcome. ¹¹ Jesus Justus too sends greetings. These are my only Jewish helpers in the work of God's kingdom; they have been a comfort to me. ¹² Greetings too from your own Epaphras, a servant of Christ Jesus, who is ever striving in prayer for you that you may stand firm in perfect fulfilment of all God's will. ¹³ I assure you that he toils mightily for you and for the brethren in Laodicea, and those in Hierapolis. ¹⁴ Our dear Luke, the doctor, greets you, as also does Demas.

¹⁵ Greetings to the brethren in Laodicea, and to Nympha and the church that meets at her house. ¹⁶ After this letter has been read out to you, have it read also in the church of

Laodicea, and obtain the letter which I have sent to Laodicea and have that read out to you. ¹⁷ Say to Archippus: 'Remember the ministry you have received in the Lord, and be sure to fulfil it. ¹⁸ I, Paul, greet you with my own hand. Remember that I am in prison. Grace be with you!

GOSPEL PASSAGES USED

OTHER "SCRIPTURE FOR MEDITATION" BOOKS

by John Bligh

1. THE INFANCY NARRATIVES. — The Infancy Narratives of St Luke and St Matthew are taken section by section. The Old Testament passages selected to go with them are those to which modern Scripture scholars have found typological allusions embedded in the actual texts of the Infancy Narratives. Father Bligh's reflections will make the reader able to see clearly what the evangelists had in mind and to catch the inspiration which they wished to impart to their readers.

2. PHILIPPIANS. — By comparing the Epistle section by section with relevant passages from the Gospels, the author demonstrates the continuity of Paul's preaching with the teaching of Christ during his ministry, and releases for the reader the power of the Spirit which is pent up in the apostle's careful chosen words. The 'Reflections' add up to a complete commentary on the Epistle. But this is more than a commentary: it places the Epistle immediately at the service of the teacher and preacher.

3. OUR DIVINE MASTER. — In this book Fr Bligh shows what Jesus taught about the various relationships which made up the structure of the world into which he was born — the relationship of God to man and man to God, of ruler to subject and subject to ruler, of Jews and non-Jews, husband and wife, parents and children, master and slave, a man and his neighbour, a man and his property (including a delightful section on Kindness to Animals).

The conclusion which emerges is that Jesus taught what are the full demands of the law of charity in each of these relationships. Any priest or teacher, confused by current controversies and efforts at renewal, and wondering what after all Christianity has to offer to our generation, will find an inspiring answer in this book.

"We know of no other popular level series in which the riches and depth of Sacred Scripture are so inspiringly revealed. The reader is given every thrill of the explorer seeking the pearl of great price." — The Irish Catholic.

ST PAUL PUBLICATIONS

An important contribution to Pauline Studies

GALATIANS
A DISCUSSION OF ST PAUL'S EPISTLE

by John Bligh

St Paul's epistle to the Galatians was written in the midst of painful controversy and has often given rise to fresh controversy among its interpreters. Jerome and Augustine disagreed over St Peter's conduct at Antioch. Luther fell in love with Galatians. The division of the western Church was consolidated by divergent interpretations of Galatians and Romans. In the present ecumenical atmosphere, it is hoped that a fresh exploration of the Epistle by a Roman Catholic scholar will help rather than hinder the movement towards reconciliation and reunion.

This commentary is addressed to a wide readership and does not assume any knowledge of the ancient languages. The author brings forth from his treasure house things both old and new. He employs the results of recent Old Testament research. He recognizes in St Paul much greater literary skill and verbal artistry than most previous commentators. And he has quarried valuable materials from Philo, Chrysostom and Jerome. Some aspects of the resulting commentary may again provoke controversy, but irenic intention is manifest — and no one will find it dull.

A short study guide is available for distribution to classes and discussion groups. In addition to the text it contains a list of questions for discussion, all of which are answered in *Galatians*.

"Brilliant, stimulating, profound, it is a work from which both amateurs and specialists have much to learn."
The Way—Oct. '69

ST PAUL PUBLICATIONS

DATE DUE

GAYLORD   PRINTED IN U.S.A.